BEST LITTLE BOOK OF BIRDS

BEST LITTLE BOOK OF BIRDS

Birds of the CHESAPEAKE BAY

Howard Youth and Gemma Radko

TIMBER PRESS
PORTLAND, OREGON

OPPOSITE: The shy American Bittern passes through and winters sparsely in the Chesapeake Bay area. It is always a lucky find.

Timber Press
Workman Publishing
Hachette Book Group, Inc.
1290 Avenue of the Americas
New York, New York 10104
timberpress.com

Timber Press is an imprint of Workman Publishing, a division of Hachette Book Group, Inc. The Timber Press name and logo are registered trademarks of Hachette Book Group, Inc.

Printed in Dongguan, China, (TLF) on responsibly sourced paper

Text and cover design by Joel Ruffier,
based on a series design by Vincent James

The publisher is not responsible for websites (or their content) that are not owned by the publisher.

ISBN 978-1-64326-415-8

A catalog record for this book is available from the Library of Congress.

To Mom and Dad, for their unwavering love and support. To Alessandra and Thomas for always being my loving kids. To Marta, for everything.
—HY

To my parents, for fostering my passion for birds, and to my husband Joseph, whose patience, love, and support continues to make it possible.
—GR

CONTENTS

Preface

My interest in birds sparked at age twelve, when I first watched herons and egrets stalk the marshes of Chincoteague National Wildlife Refuge in Virginia. There was no turning back. This birding epiphany occurred during a naturalist-led walk at the refuge, which sits just east of the Chesapeake Bay. My parents bought me my first bird guide that evening. I remember the magic of flipping through the book. Forty-eight years later, I still feel giddy thumbing through field guides, reveling in all the amazing possibilities the next birding walk might yield.

Speaking of bird walks ... about thirty years ago I was leading one at a park near my home in Silver Spring, Maryland. In the group was a birder of a similar age and experience, who became a great friend and colleague. She is the coauthor of this book. Gemma teaches ornithology courses, has been a bird bander, and is as addicted to birding as I am. She reviewed my text as I was writing it and provided key direction and revision. She is also the "eyes" on this project, selecting photos that allow the birds' beauty and distinction to speak for themselves. If a picture is worth a thousand words, you indeed have a great wealth in your hands.

Our goals here are to inspire people to enjoy the Chesapeake's dazzling avifauna and to help ensure a bright future for birds and other wildlife sharing their habitats. Wild birds need our support; in turn, their songs and activity calm and captivate us. If watching backyard birds is cathartic, seeking feathered inspiration along the Chesapeake Bay is truly "the balm."

—Howard Youth

Birding the Chesapeake Bay

The Chesapeake Bay is the largest estuary in the United States. Locals just call it "the Bay," as do I for purposes of this book. The Chesapeake is easily seen from space, resembling a jagged crocodile gape running through the state of Maryland and opening at the Atlantic in Virginia's southeast corner. Top to bottom 195 miles long, the Bay supports stunning biodiversity and more than 18 million people. It is the product of the world's second largest ocean mingling with fresh water drawn from a watershed larger than England and Wales combined. More than 150,000 miles of stream drain into it from six states and the District of Columbia.

Visitors and residents alike could spend their lifetimes exploring the rich tapestry of Chesapeake Bay landscapes and never see it all. If you enjoy watching birds and have the chance to explore this region, you will be richly rewarded. Beyond the urban waterfronts stretch vast forests, teeming marshes, swamps, and meadows. Each habitat boasts a distinctive menu of enticing birds.

Without trying hard, you'll likely see some of the Bay's spectacular birds—diving Ospreys in summer, waterfowl flocking in fall and winter, and Great Blue Herons stalking the shallows in any month. Put in some extra quality time in the field and many more exciting birds will reveal themselves.

The Bay proper, including the mouths of its major tributaries, falls within the states of Maryland (MD) and Virginia (VA), in the physiographic region called the Coastal Plain, a flat landscape of soft sediments and tidal waters. Baltimore, Maryland; Washington, DC; Wilmington, Delaware; and other cities were built on the "Fall Line," which roughly tracks the north–south I-95 highway and divides the Coastal Plain from the adjacent and rolling Piedmont Plateau to the west.

In this book, the Bay region is roughly divided into four areas: the Upper and Lower Bay (north to south) and the Eastern and Western Shores (east side and west side). The flat landscapes and coastal warmth of the Eastern Shore give this region a more southern feel, which is also apparent along both sides of the Lower Bay. Loblolly pine is prevalent, along with willow oak and sweetgum. There are also some of the northernmost bald cypress swamps, including Battle Creek Cypress Swamp in Calvert County, Maryland. At the very bottom of the Bay in southern Virginia, southern live oak and Spanish moss reach their northern limits.

By comparison, much of the Upper Bay and Western Shore features rolling terrain typical of the adjacent Piedmont, with deciduous or mixed forest with many species typical of both uplands and also riverbanks, including northern red and chestnut oaks, American beech, Virginia pine, and silver maple.

Situated midway up the Atlantic Coast, the Chesapeake Bay region enjoys four distinct seasons, offering avian delights all year. From late fall to early spring, the Chesapeake is a paradise for waterfowl, including Snow and Canada Geese, Tundra Swans, more than 25 duck species, and loons and grebes. Although songbird diversity is lower in the cold months, many species are easier to spot then because deciduous trees and shrubs are bare during this time. Many raptors also winter in the region.

Spring brings a seemingly choreographed series of migration "ripples" that start in March with an influx of northbound hawks, sparrows, and waterfowl, followed in April by the arrival of swallows and other early long-distance migrants. May marks the spring peak of songbird and shorebird migration.

Summer is the best time to see herons, egrets, ibises, terns, and pelicans, many of which nest on the Lower Bay, then often wander north during late summer and fall. The Chesapeake hosts one of the world's largest Osprey nesting populations. In summer, it seems like a "fish hawk" stick nest adorns every channel marker.

Fall migration actually begins during late summer, when southbound shorebirds start arriving after nesting on Arctic tundra and other northern habitats. Fall migration stretches longer than its spring bookend, but it's quieter: in fall, transiting songbirds don't usually sing as they do while heading northbound in spring. There are, however, more birds to see in fall, thanks to the addition of the year's crop of young birds. As in spring, fall migration comes as a series of waves, with some species arriving sooner and others later.

Accessibility

Birding hotspots mentioned in this guide are places at or near the Bay that you can visit any time and reach easily by land transport. Many of the Bay's top birding destinations have accessible trails that get birders with mobility challenges to some of the best habitats. When planning a trip, check websites of local, state, and federal parklands. On page 298 you will find a list of some recommended accessible birding sites. While strides have been made in making more green spaces accessible to all, much work remains. See birdability.org for more on this topic.

PLAN-AHEAD LOCATIONS

The Bay has some stellar limited-access sites that birders can visit if they plan ahead. Because these places are usually not open to the public, they are not mentioned elsewhere in the text. Birding is top-notch at the following sites, including the four Maryland locations where soil dredged from the Bay has been used to create wildlife habitat now managed by Maryland Environmental Service:

- Hart-Miller Island
- Cox Creek and Swan Creek Wetlands
- Masonville (adjacent Masonville Cove is open to the public)
- Poplar Island

For information on tours to the top three sites, see menv.com/service/field-trips/ and for Poplar Island, email *poplartours@menv.com*.

Craney Island Disposal Area in Portsmouth, Virginia, is an Army Corps of Engineers dredge-spoil site where limited, scheduled groups may visit, usually on weekends. To ask about Craney Island Disposal Area group access, call 757-484-1021.

Also, birders traveling by boat can view nesting birds on Martin National Wildlife Refuge, on the northern part of Smith Island, Maryland. Both Smith Island and Virginia's Tangier Island are interesting cultural, historical, and wildlife-rich places reachable by ferry.

October through February, the public can join tours to Fisherman Island National Wildlife Refuge, Virginia, which is closed during nesting season. This is the northernmost island off the Chesapeake Bay Bridge–Tunnel, where many interesting seabirds occur. Call (757) 331-3425 or (757) 331-2760.

Late April into May, male Rose-breasted Grosbeaks pass through the Bay region in crisp breeding plumage.

The iconic Snow Goose.

Bay Habitats

About half of the Chesapeake's fresh water flows in from the Susquehanna River, which also was elemental in the formation of the Bay, cutting a low-lying channel that filled after glaciers melted and sea levels rose. The water level rose over thousands of years, reaching its approximate span about 3,000 years ago. Today, its average depth is 21 feet.

ESTUARIES AND BRACKISH MARSH

Estuaries are where fresh water from rivers and streams mingles with oceanic salt water. These areas support a dizzying diversity of flora and fauna. As mentioned earlier, the Chesapeake is the largest US estuary, dominating the region's geography and nurturing many subestuaries. Open waters and associated brackish marshes dominate the Bay, providing important nurseries for shellfish, fish, birds, and other wildlife. Iconic Bay birds include wintering flocks of Canada and Snow Geese and a wide variety of duck species, loons and grebes, Great Blue Herons, Ospreys, and Bald Eagles. Find them at Sandy Point State Park, Blackwater and Eastern Neck National Wildlife Refuges, and the Chesapeake Bay Environmental Center, Maryland.

LOWER BAY SALTMARSH, ISLANDS, AND SHORELINES

Wading bird, seabird, and pelican colonies are hallmarks of the Lower Bay, where the water is salty and islands and marine-life-rich shorelines abound. Marshes in this region surge with fiddler crabs, and beaches are haunted by ghost crabs. Iconic birds of this region include the Royal Tern, Brown Pelican, Seaside Sparrow, and Boat-tailed Grackle. Winter visitors include Northern Gannet, Common Loon, and sea ducks. See them at Grandview Nature Reserve, Fort Monroe, and First Landing State Park, Virginia.

FRESHWATER MARSH

The Susquehanna, Potomac, James, and other rivers carry nutrients and sediment that flow into the Bay. Freshwater marshes fringing these tributaries provide key wildlife habitat, as do human-made freshwater impoundments managed at Blackwater National Wildlife Refuge and other areas. Key species occurring in these habitats include Wood Duck, Green Heron, Belted Kingfisher, Tree Swallow, Red-winged Blackbird, and Common Yellowthroat. See them at Blackwater National Wildlife Refuge and along the Potomac River, the Bay's second largest tributary.

SOUTHERN MIXED FOREST

The loblolly pine is a signature tree of the Eastern Shore and Lower Bay forests and is often found mixed with deciduous trees including sweetgum, willow oak, and American holly. Iconic species in this habitat include Summer Tanager, Brown-headed Nuthatch, and Pine Warbler. See them at Blackwater National Wildlife Refuge and Point Lookout State Park, Maryland, and First Landing State Park, Virginia.

The Prothonotary Warbler brightens some Bay-area swamps in spring and summer.

SWAMPS

In low spots where forest grows from just below the waterline, swamps provide rich habitats and a bounty for birders. Iconic birds of these habitats include Wood Duck, Hooded Merganser, Barred Owl, Pileated Woodpecker, and in some areas the dazzling Prothonotary Warbler. See them at First Landing State Park, Virginia, and Battle Creek Cypress Swamp, Maryland, and along Bay tributaries.

EASTERN HARDWOOD FOREST

Especially in the Upper Bay, where the Piedmont region nears the Bay shore, you will find hilly forestland more characteristic of the East's interior that includes upland tree species, such as eastern white and chestnut oaks, and those found near streamsides, including American sycamore and silver maple. Trees typically found in regrowing, young forest include tuliptree, red maple, and eastern redcedar. Iconic birds include Eastern Wood-Pewee, Red-eyed Vireo, Wood Thrush, and Red-bellied Woodpecker. See them at Elk Neck and North Point State Parks, Maryland.

MEADOWS, FALLOW FIELDS, AND SCRUBBY FOREST EDGES

Especially where invasive plants are controlled, sunny, open habitats host many birds. These "early succession" areas include many native wildflowers, shrubs, and scattered young trees. Iconic species include Orchard Oriole, Indigo Bunting, American Goldfinch, and Common Yellowthroat. See them at North Point State Park and Chesapeake Bay Environmental Center, Maryland, and Kiptopeke State Park, Virginia.

SUBURBS

Suburbs constitute a fast-growing portion of the region's land area. Neighborhoods with native trees and shrubs provide better bird habitat than those without. Native oaks, cherries, and willows, for example, host many caterpillars and other insects that songbirds need to nourish fast-growing nestlings. Iconic birds include Ruby-throated Hummingbird, Carolina Chickadee, Northern Cardinal, Blue Jay, and Northern Flicker. In open areas, nest boxes attract and benefit Eastern Bluebirds, Tree Swallows, and Purple Martins.

The Common Yellowthroat favors scrubby habitats.

Bay Conservation Issues

Indigenous and later European communities flourished across the Chesapeake, sustained by the region's abundant natural resources. At sheltered yet easily accessible Bay sites, Annapolis, Baltimore, Norfolk, and other port cities grew.

Over the decades, Bay landscapes have changed in many ways. Once-extensive wetlands and forests were filled or cleared for agriculture and suburban development. Habitat loss is one of the greatest threats to birds worldwide and this has certainly been true in the Chesapeake Bay region. Large-scale land-use changes, however, have benefited some birds. Geese and swans, for example, consume waste grains on farm fields, as do large flocks of blackbirds and starlings.

Many of the Bay's agricultural landscapes have changed in recent decades. Numerous small farms, once threaded with hedgerows, fallow fields, and woodlots, have yielded to expansive industrial-scale operations and also growing subdivisions. Casualties of these changes

A Dunlin strides the shallows.

The Bay's smallest woodpecker, the Downy.

include the Northern Bobwhite and American Kestrel, which are now scarce nesters, and the Eastern Meadowlark, which is in steep decline.

Over the last 50 years, areas of submerged aquatic vegetation (SAV) in the Bay have severely diminished, mainly due to agricultural runoff and sedimentation. SAV maintains good water quality, absorbs excess nutrients, reduces erosion, and helps to maintain healthy levels of oxygen in the Bay. It also provides key habitat for fish, crabs, and other aquatic life, and sustenance for wintering flocks of Canvasback, American Coot, and other birds.

In addition to habitat loss and agricultural runoff, the Bay region is feeling the effects of climate-driven coastline loss, particularly on islands and along the Eastern Shore.

Despite these threats and much work left to do, there has been progress in conserving the Bay. The Chesapeake was one of the world's first estuaries to be the focus of large-scale restoration efforts, which are ongoing. Its environmental challenges are well known to the public, and decades of conservation work have yielded successes, including strides in recovering SAV and oyster beds in some areas and the strong rebound of Bald Eagle and Eastern Bluebird populations. Protection of nesting waterbird and seabird colonies, especially on the Lower Bay, no doubt helped welcome two recent breeding arrivals, the Brown Pelican and White Ibis, although steady losses of shoreline threaten to erase some of these gains.

Continuous and thoughtful conservation planning and action, fueled by strong public support, will be key in ensuring a bright future for the Bay's bird populations.

A juvenile Osprey surveys its watery surroundings.

How to Help Bay Birds

Here are some ways you can help birds of the Chesapeake Bay and its watershed:

DO NOT wash chemicals (such as those in fertilizers, pesticides, oil, or paint) into street drains.

PLANT NATIVE shrubs, trees, and wildflowers.

LEARN TO identify invasive introduced plants and work to control them in your yard and, where permitted, in nearby areas.

CATS KILL approximately 2.4 billion wild birds each year in the United States, according to American Bird Conservancy (abcbirds.org). Keeping your cat indoors protects birds and other wildlife, while keeping your pet safe.

TAKE STEPS to reduce fatal bird-glass collisions, cutting reflection on exterior glass by, for example, adhering closely spaced decals. For tips, see abcbirds.org/glass-collisions

PROVIDE a water feature safe from cats and away from reflective windows, where birds can drink and bathe.

DON'T USE pesticides, to protect both birds and their food sources. Most songbirds, for example, rely upon large numbers of insects, including caterpillars, to feed their young.

IF YOU feed birds, regularly clean feeders (and bird baths) with a mild bleach solution, then rinse thoroughly and let them dry, to reduce chances of disease transmission.

WHERE SAFE, leave dead or dying trees or "install" large woody snags. Birds use these to view their surroundings, sing, and nest (woodpeckers, bluebirds, etc.).

INSTALL and maintain nest boxes for cavity nesters including Purple Martins, Tree Swallows, Eastern Bluebirds, American Kestrels, Eastern Screech-Owls, and Wood Ducks.

Gear and Safety

You're a birder if you find yourself interested in watching and identifying birds. To start, all you really need is to see or hear what's around you, then consult a field guide or birding app to identify the birds you found. You'll come across the largest variety of species by visiting a range of habitats. Many birds get up early, so being an "early bird" yourself is usually a helpful strategy.

Most birders carry a comfortable, clear pair of binoculars. Others also invest in a spotting scope to scan distant mudflats, open water, and treetops. A lightweight camera with a versatile zoom is a very handy accessory for documenting unusual birds.

Keeping notes on the birds you see helps you remember what you saw, and where. You can easily do this on your phone or computer, sharing your sightings and photos on databases such as eBird (eBird.org). Apps including Merlin (merlin.allaboutbirds.org) can help you identify the birds you hear and see.

Spring and fall in the Chesapeake Bay region often seem fleeting, sandwiched between prolonged summer mugginess and winter chill. How you "weather the weather" can often dictate how long you stay outdoors enjoying birds. Keep a close eye on the day's forecast, so you can dress in layers that allow you to stay comfortable in the field.

Pack water, sunscreen, a wide-brimmed hat (or knit hat in winter), repellent, and sandwiches and snacks. Before stepping out, you also might want to check the "bird forecast": weather radar is now used to predict and monitor ebbs and flows of bird migration. For example, see Cornell Lab of Ornithology's BirdCast website at birdcast.info.

Many birders wear lightweight, wicking long pants and long sleeves in spring and summer. The sun is not the only reason. Poison ivy, which has glossy three-part leaves, occurs both on the ground and in trees. Poison oak is similar but is a shrub. In most people, contact with these plants can cause a diabolically itchy, bumpy rash that can take weeks to fade. (Best to learn to identify and avoid these plants.) Also, ticks are often present, especially in tall grass. They can carry several diseases including Lyme disease. At the start of your walk, an application of repellent at the tops of shoes and pant cuffs can help. Also, after each outing, plan on checking for ticks, showering using a washcloth, and not wearing field clothes again before washing them.

Depending upon location, habitat, and season, mosquitoes and biting flies can also be a nuisance, especially on still, humid days from late May well into September.

The region hosts many interesting snake species. Three are venomous. Seldom seen, the eastern copperhead lives around stone walls, brush piles, and tangles. Much more localized, the northern cottonmouth and the "canebrake" timber rattlesnake only occur near the bottom of the Bay in southeastern Virginia.

A singing male Prairie Warbler.

Staying on wide trails and watching where you step are the best precautions to keep you away from snakes, ticks, and poison ivy. (Also watch for poison ivy branches stretching out from tree trunks.) Added benefits of staying on trails include reducing the chance of spreading invasive plant seeds via shoes and minimizing erosion and other disturbance to wildlife and habitat.

Birding often takes us to unusual, isolated, and captivating settings. Wherever you choose to go, always follow your instincts and put safety first.

Male Long-tailed Ducks.

A male Eastern Bluebird.

A Black-necked Stilt.

Birding Ethics

Careless birding can harm wildlife and habitats. But if you prioritize the interest and safety of the birds, it's easy to watch them in a sustainable and highly enjoyable way. Here are some points to consider:

MINIMIZE OR REFRAIN from playing bird sound recordings to lure in birds, especially during nesting season and in regard to sensitive/scarce species. Many public areas like national parks and national wildlife refuges prohibit the use of playback.

DON'T APPROACH birds so closely that they begin to act differently in your presence. Strive to leave birds and their habitats as you find them.

LEARN TO bird by ear. Knowing calls and songs of common birds enables you to bird more thoroughly, and "count" birds you know you heard, instead of having to chase down shy species.

DON'T PUBLICIZE vulnerable nest sites or roosting owl locations, which could result in increased stress or risk of predation to these birds.

OBEY SIGNAGE and *never trespass*, both on private property and in parts of public areas marked off-limits (including areas fenced to protect beach-nesting birds).

SHARE YOUR ENTHUSIASM and sightings with people of all backgrounds, ages, and abilities. Inclusion and encouragement spread the joy and nurture conservation-minded nature lovers.

SEE THE American Birding Association's complete birding code of ethics at aba.org/aba-code-of-birding-ethics.

A male Summer Tanager.

An Eastern Screech-Owl.

An Eastern Kingbird.

Using This Book

This book is intended to be easy to use. It focuses on 124 "core" bird species you are likely to see or hear while exploring the Bay region. In the accounts, many similar species are shown, with identification tips for differentiating them.

Scientists classify the world's living things using scientific names in Latin and Greek, organizing their relationships through a field of study called taxonomy. Genetic, anatomical, and behavioral similarities help define related bird families, which are made of related genera (singular genus), which in turn are made up of individual species.

A species is a distinct population that usually does not hybridize with other species.

Each species is assigned a two-part scientific name: the first (capitalized) part denotes the genus, followed by the individual species name in lowercase. For example, the Carolina Chickadee is called *Poecile carolinensis*. While other chickadees share the genus name *Poecile*, only the Carolina has the species name *carolinensis*.

Although in this book most bird species appear in taxonomic or scientific order, some unrelated "look-alike" birds (the ducks, grebes, loons, and coots and the swifts and swallows, for example) are presented near each other for ease of comparison. Photo pages include an image of an adult bird and often a shot of an immature or similar species for comparison.

Each species entry provides the following specifics:

PHOTOS
to help you to confirm your identification visually and appreciate the beauty of each species.

CAPTION
mentions the sex and characteristics of the species shown.

COMMON NAME

Scientific Name Size of the bird in length (head to tail) and wingspan

APPEARANCE Size, plumage color, bill shape, and other diagnostic markings. These descriptions are essential for precise identification in the field.

HABITAT AND BEHAVIOR Habitats the bird frequents in the Chesapeake Bay region, what it eats, nesting behavior if it breeds in the region, and other distinctive behaviors.

YEARLY ABUNDANCE When and where to find the bird and how common it is around the Bay. This includes information on how likely you are to find each species during the months or seasons indicated. Sites listed are open to the public. These are by no means the only places to find each species, but they are good places to look. Broad categories of frequency include rare, scarce, uncommon, common, and very common.

SOUNDS Typical sounds given by the species while in the region. Songs are complex sounds used for territorial defense or courtship, while calls are usually shorter sounds used in alarm or for contact.

SIMILAR SPECIES Birds with similar appearance that could be confused for the featured species.

Bird Family Descriptions

A family is a grouping of related genera (singular genus), with each genus containing closely related species. The following descriptions focus only on families of bird species featured in this book and are listed in the order they appear on these pages.

GEESE, SWANS & DUCKS (family Anatidae)

Gifted with strong flight, broad bills, and webbed feet, these social birds deftly navigate air, land, and water and are an indelible part of the Chesapeake scene from fall into spring. During that time, birders journeying across the region can spot 30 or more species that belong to this family.

GREBES (family Podicipedidae)

Although not closely related, grebes are similar in appearance to loons, with straight, pointy bills, and legs set back on their bodies. Like loons, they dive, then pop back up not far away. From a distance, they can be easily overlooked as ducks.

LOONS (family Gaviidae)

Loons are large birds that resemble low-slung, dagger-billed ducks. With legs set far back on their bodies and large webbed feet, they are agile divers, pursuing fish and other aquatic life. This arrangement, however, makes it very awkward for them to move on land.

COOTS & RAILS (family Rallidae)

This family of wetland birds includes some of the most elusive birds in the world (the rails) and among the easiest to see (coots and gallinules). Rails slowly walk within hidden seams in thick wetland vegetation, compressing their feathers and stretching to navigate tight spaces and be "thin as rails." In contrast, coots gather in flocks, swimming in open waters and diving with the aid of wide, lobed feet.

TURKEYS (family Phasianidae)

Turkeys share this family with other upland game birds including grouse, ptarmigans, and pheasants. Wild Turkeys often roost in trees and spend their days quietly strolling the forest floor and fields in search of tree nuts and grains.

OYSTERCATCHERS (family Haematopodidae)

Large, boldly colored, and loud, the American Oystercatcher is the only member of this family found in the East. It uses its colorful chisel-like bill to open shellfish but also grabs worms and other invertebrates. In the region, it mainly occurs in the Lower Bay.

PLOVERS (family Charadriidae)

Plovers haunt open areas, most often mudflats or other shallow wet habitats. The Killdeer occurs in short-grass fields and pastures as well. In breeding plumage, the region's plovers all have boldly marked heads and necks. Although similar to sandpipers, plovers stand out thanks to their rather blocky heads, thick and rather short bills, and habit of feeding in a start-and-stop fashion.

SANDPIPERS (family Scolopacidae)

Varied in bill shape, body size, and feeding style, migrating sandpipers stop and mingle in very shallow water and on mudflats. Dunlin and a few others brave Bay winters, and a few species breed in the region, including the Willet and American Woodcock. Some Bay islands and dredge-spoil sites and many Atlantic Coast sites host large concentrations of migrating sandpipers, but birders should watch for these exciting birds anywhere in the Bay region.

GULLS & TERNS (family Laridae)

Gulls feed in a variety of ways, snatching small animals, carrion, or other foods from land, shore, and the water's surface. With angular wings and pointy bills, terns dip and dive to snag fish. Gulls and terns usually nest in colonies, benefiting from safety in numbers in the open areas where they lay their eggs.

GANNETS & BOOBIES (Sulidae)

Northern Gannets return to Canadian breeding colonies in spring, but spend much of their lives wandering the Atlantic (and also the Bay's open waters). Gannets and boobies have long, narrow wings that they fold tight against their bodies while plunging, dart-like, into waters rich in fish and squid. The Brown Booby is a rare straggler to the Bay during months when gannets are scarce or absent.

CORMORANTS (family Phalacrocoracidae)

When flying in loose formation, these dark, long-necked birds can be confused for geese. In the water, cormorants are low-slung and snake-necked, somewhat like loons. Like loons, they dive for fish and other prey, thrust downward by their wide webbed feet. On land, cormorants stand upright, often spreading their wings to facilitate drying.

PELICANS (family Pelecanidae)

This charismatic group of large waterbirds is well known for gathering fish in their throat pouches. Each species hunts in a different way. The Brown Pelican now nests on the Lower Bay, where it is frequently seen gliding over the water, then wheeling and diving to scoop up fish near the water's surface.

HERONS & EGRETS (family Ardeidae)

This family of elegant, long-necked wading birds hunts fish and other wetland life by wading or waiting, then striking with "spring-loaded" neck thrusts. The region hosts 11 species, each with its own feeding style. The Great Blue Heron is the largest and most widespread species.

IBISES (family Threskiornithidae)

These curve-billed wading birds inhabit coastal marshes and other soggy, open areas. The White Ibis is a recent and increasing addition to the Bay's avifauna, joining the Glossy Ibis as an exciting bird to see on the Lower Bay.

VULTURES (family Cathartidae)

Among the most common of the region's soaring birds, vultures are the "cleanup crew" of the bird world, dining almost exclusively on carrion. They lack the strong talons of hawks and eagles. Two species are commonly found in the Bay region.

OSPREYS (family Pandionidae)

This family contains just one species. The Osprey is found on all continents save Antarctica and is regarded by many as the ultimate fishing bird. After hovering high over the water, an Osprey dives feetfirst to grapple large fish with its formidable talons. This species' large stick nests are a familiar sight across the Bay.

HAWKS & EAGLES (family Accipitridae)

Hook-billed and clawed, these well-equipped raptors range from the dove-sized Sharp-shinned Hawk to the mighty Bald Eagle. They hunt in various ways, including straight-line attacks and swoops from high above.

FALCONS (family Falconidae)

Although they are raptors, falcons are not closely related to hawks, eagles, ospreys, vultures, or owls. These fast-flying, pointy-winged birds ambush or dive on a wide variety of avian species, including birds their size or even larger.

OWLS (family Strigidae)

The region hosts up to eight owl species; three are widespread residents. Built for stealth and action in the dark, owls have disk-shaped faces, keen vision and hearing, and formidable talons. Due to their nocturnal habits, most of the Bay's owls are seen infrequently.

DOVES & PIGEONS (family Columbidae)

Doves and pigeons have smallish, rounded heads and robust bodies. They spend much time walking on the ground in search of seeds and grains. Mourning Doves often nest near people, placing loosely assembled stick nests in trees, shrubs, and planters.

CUCKOOS (family Cuculidae)

In other parts of the world, cuckoos are famed for laying their eggs in nests of other bird species. North American cuckoos only do this on occasion, although they may regularly deposit eggs in nests of others of their own kind. The two species that occur in the region are sleek and long tailed, and adept at slinking through foliage in search of caterpillars and other prey.

HUMMINGBIRDS (family Trochilidae)

High-octane sprites, hummingbirds are the Bay's smallest and perhaps most celebrated backyard birds. One species nests in the East; a few others turn up occasionally during the fall and winter. Hummingbirds use their long, thin bills to probe nectar-bearing blooms and to snatch tiny invertebrates. Their wings revolve in a figure-eight motion too fast for eyes to see, and allow these birds to hover in midair and even fly backward.

KINGFISHERS (family Alcedinidae)

Kingfishers have blocky heads and daggerlike bills. They dive for fish and other aquatic creatures and nest in tunnels in eroded banks. The Belted Kingfisher is the region's only representative of this flashy family.

WOODPECKERS (family Picidae)

Woodpeckers shimmy up tree trunks, braced by stiff tail feathers. Strong neck and head muscles allow them to hammer against decaying wood to find food, and to telegraph their presence to others of their kind. Woodpeckers excavate nest cavities in dead or dying trees. Seven species occur around the Bay; an eighth, the rare Red-cockaded Woodpecker, gets close, occurring at a few sites in southern Virginia.

FLYCATCHERS (family Tyrannidae)

These active birds only occur in the Americas, where their family is the largest, containing more than 440 species. In the Chesapeake Bay region, five species are widespread nesters. Flycatchers hunt from perches, sometimes glean branches, or drop down to the ground to grab insects and other invertebrates. Most leave the region in fall, returning in April or May.

VIREOS (family Vireonidae)

Easily mistaken for similar-sized warblers, vireos have thicker bills and more deliberate movements. Most stay under cover and sing persistently during the nesting season. These birds leave the Bay area for warmer climes each fall.

JAYS & CROWS (family Corvidae)

One jay, two crows, and a raven comprise the Bay's cast of corvids. These intelligent, adaptable, and omnivorous birds inhabit a wide variety of habitats, often feeding and nesting in cities and suburbs.

CHICKADEES & TITMICE (family Paridae)

Active, curious, and gregarious, these songbirds form the nucleus of mixed-species flocks. Neither the Carolina Chickadee nor the Tufted Titmouse migrates. They thrive in woodlands throughout the region, nesting in small cavities in dead or dying wood, and sometimes in nest boxes.

LARKS (family Alaudidae)

There are more than 90 lark species found worldwide, but just one is native to the Americas. Famed for their aerial songs and flight displays, larks are also notorious skulkers. The Horned Lark is common in Bay country but is often overlooked, as it hides in plain sight on sparsely vegetated or bare expanses of farmland.

SWIFTS (family Apodidae)

Just one swift species occurs in the East. Although in flight Chimney Swifts somewhat resemble swallows, they are not related. Unlike swallows, swifts cannot perch on wires or branches. Their tiny, rake-like feet can only grasp rough vertical surfaces, such as chimney bricks. They feed on flying insects captured on the wing.

SWALLOWS & MARTINS

(family Hirundinidae)

These aerial insectivores frequent open areas, often near water. Six species occur in the region. While often seen overhead, these agile birds also readily perch on wires, tall reeds, and tree snags. Purple Martins and Tree Swallows often use nest boxes put out for them. A few Tree Swallows usually ride out winter along the Lower Bay.

KINGLETS (family Regulidae)

Along with the Winter Wren, the two kinglets are the smallest birds found in the Bay region during the winter. Round-bodied and short-tailed, they hover at branch tips and glean tiny insects along thin branches. They often join mixed-species flocks that include chickadees and titmice.

WAXWINGS (family Bombycillidae)

These sleek, crested songbirds are usually seen in flocks that wander in search of fruiting trees, including mulberries, hollies, and cedars. They are named for the red, waxlike deposits on their wing feathers.

NUTHATCHES (family Sittidae)

Nuthatches have flat-crowned heads, chisel-like bills, short tails, and large feet that enable them to clamber up and down tree trunks, work along branches, or clamp onto pine cones. Three species occur in the region.

CREEPERS (family Certhiidae)

The only member of its family in North America, the Brown Creeper occurs across the region fall to spring (rarely nesting). This bird's cryptic back pattern helps it blend with the trunks it creeps around as it searches for spiders and other tiny prey. Unlike nuthatches, it can only creep one way—up.

GNATCATCHERS (family Polioptilidae)

Tiny and super-active, gnatcatchers cock their tails and constantly call in thin, lisping tones as they forage for small invertebrates among the leaves. They construct compact cup nests made of plant bits, spiderwebs, and lichens.

WRENS (family Troglodytidae)

Lurking in the foliage but often revealing their presence with loud songs and calls, these small songbirds can be distinguished by their thin, slightly downcurved bills and jauntily cocked tails.

CATBIRDS, THRASHERS & MOCKINGBIRDS (family Mimidae)

Capable mimics of other birds but also composing their own "lyrics," the Brown Thrasher, Gray Catbird, and Northern Mockingbird are each found in a slightly different habitat.

STARLINGS (family Sturnidae)

European Starlings spread across the continent after being introduced in New York City in the late 1800s. They nest in cavities, often outcompeting native species. Starlings have long, pointed bills and shorter tails than the blackbirds with which they often mingle in huge fall and winter flocks. In breeding plumage, both sexes sport yellow bills and iridescent plumage; in winter, they are dark-billed and dotted with white spots.

THRUSHES (family Turdidae)

This widespread family includes some of the region's most out-in-the-open species (the robin and bluebird) and some of its most retiring (the brown-backed thrushes). Thrushes forage on the ground and in fruiting trees, shrubs, and vines. They are known for their rich vocal repertoires.

FINCHES (family Fringillidae)

Usually found in small groups, these thick-billed songbirds focus much of their attention on seeds and fruits, which they even feed to their nestlings (most songbirds primarily feed invertebrates to their growing young). Some of the region's most familiar feeder birds belong to this family. In the field, their rich songs and calls easily draw attention to these distinctive birds.

OLD WORLD SPARROWS (family Passeridae)

A bit huskier and thicker billed than native sparrows, the introduced House Sparrow now thrives alongside humans on six continents. House Sparrows stuff their nests in crevices in buildings and also compete with native species for nest boxes and natural cavity nest sites.

NEW WORLD SPARROWS & TOWHEES (family Passerellidae)

This family occurs only in the Americas. In the region, it includes almost 20 small, streaky brown or plain-breasted songbirds and the larger, boldly patterned Eastern Towhee. Field marks, habitats, habits, and songs differ between species. With practice, identifying birds in this group is not as daunting as it may seem.

MEADOWLARKS, ORIOLES & BLACKBIRDS (family Icteridae)

Another Americas-only family, this group includes the blackbirds, grackles, cowbirds, bobolinks, meadowlarks, and New World orioles, which got their name from their similar appearance to unrelated orioles found from Europe to Australia. Most are medium-sized songbirds with sleek outlines and long, pointy bills. Outside nesting season, blackbirds, grackles, and cowbirds assemble in large, often mixed flocks that frequent the region's farmlands.

WARBLERS (family Parulidae)

This large New World family of energetic, colorful, and vociferous songbirds is among the most thrilling to birders. Each year, 35 species occur in the region, most passing through during migration. Warblers have thin, tweezer-like bills perfect for grasping caterpillars and other small invertebrate prey. Some are strongly sexually dimorphic (males and females have different plumages). Many wear their brightest colors in spring and summer.

TANAGERS, CARDINALS & NEW WORLD BUNTINGS (family Cardinalidae)

This family includes some of the region's most colorful birds. Tanagers have stout bills used to pluck berries and capture large insects such as wasps. Cardinals, buntings, and grosbeaks have thick, cone-shaped bills perfect for cracking seeds.

FIELD GUIDE

Adult white morph.
Medium-sized white goose with black wingtips and pink legs and bill.

Adult dark morph.
Note white head and neck, and pink bill.

Ross's Goose.
Ross's has similar coloration but is smaller, with a stubbier bill that lacks the black "grin stripe" seen on Snow Geese.

SNOW GOOSE

Anser caerulescens Length: 31" / Wingspan: 56"

After nesting on the Arctic tundra, thousands of these striking birds fly south to winter in the Bay region. Gleaming white flocks descend upon farm fields and wetlands like avian snow showers. Dark birds often pepper these flocks—all-dark immatures and "blue geese," a dark-bodied, white-headed color morph.

Forages in wetlands and farm fields, feeding on grasses, sedges, waste grain, and other plant matter.

Look for them at Blackwater National Wildlife Refuge and Great Marsh Park in Cambridge, MD; in Virginia, the best spot is east of the Bay at Chincoteague National Wildlife Refuge. Flocks wander. Locally common November–March.

Most common call a bark-like, flat *kowk!*

Smaller Ross's Goose is rare, usually found among Snow or Canada Goose flocks.

Adult.
Large, brown-bodied goose with black head and neck and white cheeks.

Cackling Goose.
Plumage similar to Canada but bird is smaller, with stubby bill, shorter neck, and squarish head shape.

Brant.
Small, dark goose with blackish chest, neck, and head. Lacks white cheeks but has faint white collar.

CANADA GOOSE

Branta canadensis

Length: 45" / Wingspan: 60"

Fall through winter, most large flocks of this familiar wild goose consist of migratory Canada-nesting birds. However, resident Canada Geese are also present year-round.

Wetlands, drainage ponds, farm fields, golf courses, and parks. Eats grasses, grains, and other plant matter. The nest, placed along the water's edge, is made of sticks, marsh grass, and other vegetation, and lined with down.

Look for them at any of the region's wildlife refuges or state parks. Very common October–March. Resident birds start nesting in March.

Familiar, plaintive honk that echoes across open expanses.

Cackling Goose is a scarce fall and winter visitor, usually found among Canada Geese. Brant is a common winter visitor at the mouth of the Bay, at areas like Fort Monroe, VA.

Adult.
Large and all white, with long neck and black bill. Note yellow lores (area between eye and bill), though some birds lack this coloration.

Mute Swan.
Distinctive orange bill with black mask and knob. Neck usually held in S shape.

Trumpeter Swans.
Coloration like Tundra but larger. Never has yellow on lores. Long, uncurved bill profile.

TUNDRA SWAN

Cygnus columbianus Length: 52" / Wingspan: 75"

Soft, hooting calls overhead hail the fall return of these elegant all-white birds.

Marshes and farm fields. In the Bay region, feeds on waste grain, including corn and soybean, as well as aquatic vegetation.

Look for them at Blackwater and Eastern Neck National Wildlife Refuges, MD. Near the Bay in VA, two reliable places are Back Bay and Chincoteague National Wildlife Refuges. Common but somewhat localized, November–March.

Soft, sad-sounding *hoot* or *pa-loo*, very different from Snow Goose's bark and Canada Goose's honk.

The introduced Mute Swan is a patchily distributed resident; the larger, reintroduced Trumpeter Swan is scarce. See also Snow Goose (page 50).

Breeding male (bottom) and female (top).
Male has backswept crest, red-orange bill, bold black-and-white head pattern, brick-colored chest, and yellow sides. Female has distinctive white teardrop around eye and boxy head with short crest.

WOOD DUCK

Aix sponsa Length: 18.5" / Wingspan: 30"

Named for its tree-nesting habits, the eye-popping drake (male) resembles a richly painted decoy. Unlike other North American ducks, this local breeder often nests twice a year.

Swamps and along marsh edges. Diet includes aquatic plants, seeds, and tree nuts such as acorns and beechnuts. Also consumes some insects and other invertebrates. Nest, lined with down feathers, sits within a large tree cavity or nest box.

Look for them at North Point State Park, Eastern Neck National Wildlife Refuge, and Chesapeake Bay Environmental Center, MD, and at Stumpy Lake Natural Area, VA. Much of the year, particularly common along main tributaries including the Potomac and James Rivers; scarce January–February.

Female utters wailing *woo-eep*. Male gives rising whistle.

See Hooded Merganser (page 84).

Breeding male (bottom) and female (top).
Male has dark green head, white chest, and rusty sides. Female brown with outsized orange bill.

NORTHERN SHOVELER

Spatula clypeata Length: 19" / Wingspan: 30"

This distinctive duck patrols tranquil marsh waters, straining food from the water with its disproportionately long bill.

Along marsh, pond, and cove edges scouring the water's surface and below for seeds and marsh plant bits, as well as tiny aquatic invertebrates. Rarely tips its rear end up like a Mallard does.

Look for them at Blackwater National Wildlife Refuge, MD, along with various Virginia Beach sites at the Bay's mouth. At times, at Chesapeake Bay Environmental Center, MD. Fairly common September–April.

Females utter flat quack and *gek gek gek gek* calls. Males often silent on wintering grounds.

See Mallard (under American Black Duck on page 64) and Gadwall (page 60). Female Mallard and female Gadwall lack the outsized bill.

Breeding female (left) and male (right).
Male mostly gray, with thin black bill and black rear end. Female's bill two-toned: blackish above and orange below. Both sexes have white wing patches.

GADWALL

Mareca strepera Length: 20" / Wingspan: 33"

Understated yet distinctive, the Gadwall is easily overlooked among mixed flocks of flashier species. The male's grayish body and head contrast sharply with its black rear.

Favors shallow waters, often tipping its rear end up as Mallards do, mainly to reach aquatic plant leaves and stems.

Look for them at Grandview Nature Preserve, VA, and at North Point and Sandy Point State Parks, Eastern Neck National Wildlife Refuge, and Chesapeake Environmental Center, MD. Fairly common to common October–April. A scarce breeder in the region.

Male utters almost treefrog-like *deh deh deh*. Females quack. Both genders chatter while feeding.

Female Mallard and Northern Shoveler have larger bills and thicker necks. In flight, watch for Gadwall's white square in back flight feathers, called secondaries.

Breeding male (left) and female (right). Male has white "pate" and green mask and back of neck. Also note small gray bill and male's white flank and black tail. Female has buffy body, speckled grayish head, and small gray bill.

Breeding male Eurasian Wigeon. Rusty head and chest and cream-colored "pate."

AMERICAN WIGEON

Mareca americana

Length: 20" / Wingspan: 32"

The male's green mask contrasts with his gleaming white crown, a feature that earned it the folk name "Baldpate." Sometimes elusive as they quietly feed among marsh grasses and within mixed duck flocks. Male and female appear rather blunt headed, thanks to smallish gray bills and rounded foreheads.

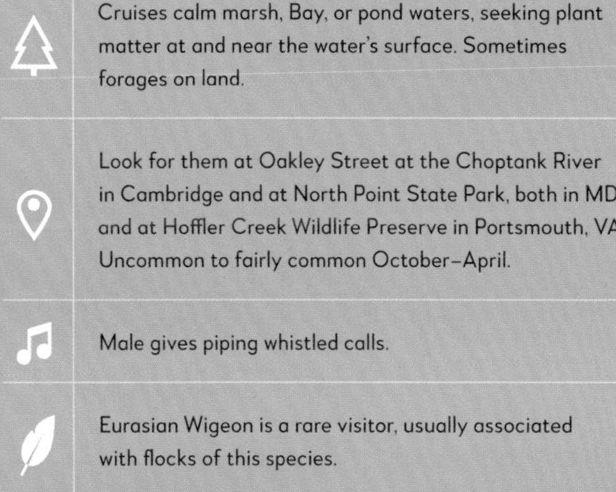

Cruises calm marsh, Bay, or pond waters, seeking plant matter at and near the water's surface. Sometimes forages on land.

Look for them at Oakley Street at the Choptank River in Cambridge and at North Point State Park, both in MD, and at Hoffler Creek Wildlife Preserve in Portsmouth, VA. Uncommon to fairly common October–April.

Male gives piping whistled calls.

Eurasian Wigeon is a rare visitor, usually associated with flocks of this species.

Male (right) and female (left).
Both have these field marks: dark body, pale head and neck, and blue wing patches that lack white borders. Male's bill is yellow; female's is dull olive.

Female Mallard.
Brown body with dark scalloping and orange bill with dark bar in middle. Blue wing patch with white borders.

AMERICAN BLACK DUCK

Anas rubripes

Length: 23" / Wingspan: 35"

This dark-bodied eastern duck is one of the Bay's most characteristic species, along with the blue crab, eastern oyster, striped bass, and Canvasback.

Freshwater and brackish wetlands, but favors saltmarsh. Eats seeds, leaves, and other plant matter, but also mollusks, crustaceans, and insects. The nest is placed on a bank or island, at a wetland's edge, or atop a vacant duck blind.

Look for them at Eastern Neck and Blackwater National Wildlife Refuges and the Chesapeake Bay Environmental Center, MD, and the Eastern Shore of Virginia National Wildlife Refuge and Messick Point, VA. Has declined due to habitat loss, coastline change, and hybridization with related Mallards. Northern birds boost Bay numbers fall through late winter. Fairly common year-round.

Familiar quack, similar to that of Mallard.

The familiar Mallard drake is distinctive, but see female Mallard.

Breeding male (right) and female (left).
Male has long tail (longer plume often present but not shown here). His chocolate-brown head contrasts with white on the long neck. Female has buffy head, long neck, and thin, slate-colored bill.

NORTHERN PINTAIL

Anas acuta Length: 21" / Wingspan: 34"

Elongated and sleek, this duck stands out in a crowd thanks to the male's distinctive chocolate-brown head and long black tail.

Found in flocks in marshes, on lakes, and in flooded fields. Dabbles, submerges its head, or walks along edges to find seeds and insects.

Look for them at Blackwater and Eastern Neck National Wildlife Refuges and Chesapeake Bay Environmental Center, MD, and at Magothy Bay Natural Area Preserve, VA. Fairly common locally, late October–March.

Resonant, blurry *brrrr* and sliding, breezy *wiiizzeh*.

See female Gadwall (page 60) and female Mallard (under American Black Duck on page 64).

Breeding male.
Bronzy head with green mask. Vertical white bar on side. Black-and-buff tail.

Adult female.
Dark brown with round head and small bill. Cream stripe on tail. Green wing patch (not always visible).

Adult female Blue-winged Teal.
Lighter brown above, with longer bill and whitish particularly on throat and behind bill. Pale blue wing patches in flight.

GREEN-WINGED TEAL

Anas crecca Length: 14.5" / Wingspan: 23"

This compact duck is the Bay's smallest non-diving duck and is found in pairs or flocks, both in shallows and on shorelines. In all plumages, these birds reveal a striking buff-and-black tail pattern. At close range, the distinctive males are a feast for the eyes.

Marshes, ponds, and flooded fields.

Look for them at Magothy Bay Natural Area Preserve and Pleasure House Point Natural Area, VA, and at Blackwater and Eastern Neck National Wildlife Refuges, MD. Fairly common mid-August–April.

Ringing whistles and peeps.

Blue-winged Teal is fairly common in the region during migration but scarce in winter.

Breeding male.
Sloped forehead, with black bill and chest and reddish head. White body.

Female.
Sloped forehead; all-black bill. Tan head and light gray body clouded with diffuse brown.

Males and female (center) Redheads.
Male has gray body, red head, and pale blue bill tipped with black. Female has round, brown head the same color as body, and gray bill tipped with black.

CANVASBACK

Aythya valisineria Length: 21" / Wingspan: 29"

The Chesapeake Bay is an important wintering area for this distinctive species, but these days annual winter counts yield far fewer birds than in decades past. The drop coincided with a steep decline in submerged aquatic vegetation.

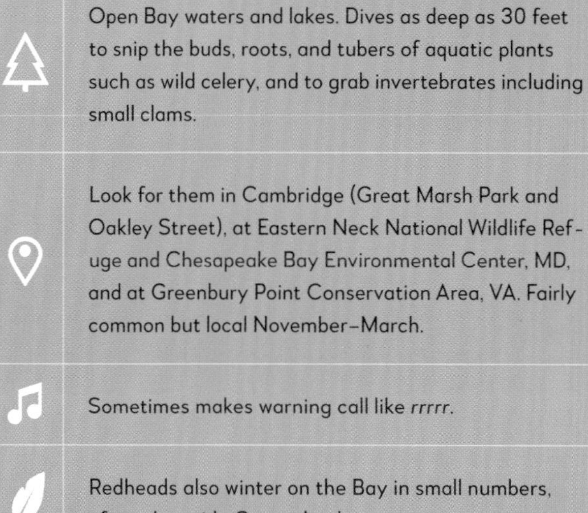

Open Bay waters and lakes. Dives as deep as 30 feet to snip the buds, roots, and tubers of aquatic plants such as wild celery, and to grab invertebrates including small clams.

Look for them in Cambridge (Great Marsh Park and Oakley Street), at Eastern Neck National Wildlife Refuge and Chesapeake Bay Environmental Center, MD, and at Greenbury Point Conservation Area, VA. Fairly common but local November–March.

Sometimes makes warning call like *rrrrr*.

Redheads also winter on the Bay in small numbers, often alongside Canvasbacks.

Breeding male.
White crescent "blaze" on side and two white bands on bill. Male's black head, chest, back, and tail contrast with gray sides.

Female.
Whitish around eye and behind bill. Gray bill with black tip—these colors usually separated by thin white band.

RING-NECKED DUCK

Aythya collaris Length: 17" / Wingspan: 25"

The drake “ringneck” looks touched up with bold highlights. The white crescent between its chest and sides and the two white bill stripes are handy field marks. The male’s bronzy collar, for which the species is named, is not easy to see in the field.

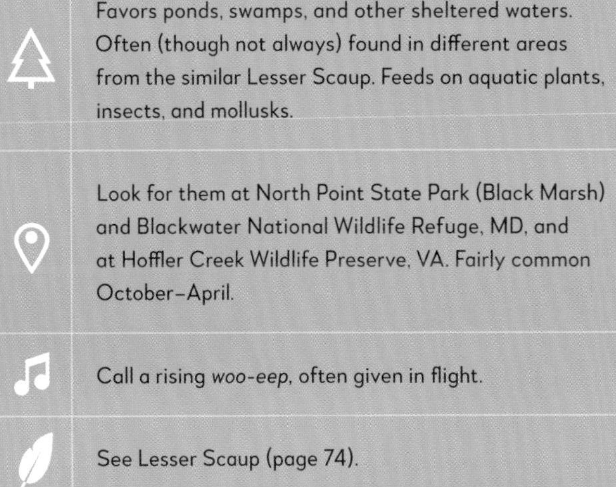

Favors ponds, swamps, and other sheltered waters. Often (though not always) found in different areas from the similar Lesser Scaup. Feeds on aquatic plants, insects, and mollusks.

Look for them at North Point State Park (Black Marsh) and Blackwater National Wildlife Refuge, MD, and at Hoffler Creek Wildlife Preserve, VA. Fairly common October–April.

Call a rising *woo-eep*, often given in flight.

See Lesser Scaup (page 74).

Breeding male.
All-dark head often shows slight peak toward back end. Generally thinner necked than Greater, but this is often hard to see except under close comparison. At close range, "nail" at bill tip often smaller than in Greater.

Female.
Head often peaked toward back. Similar female Greater Scaup (not shown) has rounder head, thicker neck, and, at close range, broader bill with larger black "nail" at tip.

Breeding male Greater Scaup.
Thick hindneck/back of head. Head often appears rounder and more bulged over forehead than in Lesser. Greater has broader bill, often evident at close range, as is larger black "nail" at bill tip.

LESSER SCAUP

Aythya affinis

Length: 16.5" / Wingspan: 25"

Telling Lesser from Greater Scaups is tricky. Both occur in the Bay, often together. Side by side and at close range, Lessers appear thinner necked, often show a slight peak at the back of the head, and have narrower bills with smaller black "nails" at the bill tip. (Greaters often appear more "filled out" or blocky at back of head.) At a distance, you may not be able to separate these species with confidence.

Common in sheltered coves, lakes, and large ponds. Dives for its food, which includes snails, clams, crustaceans, some insects, and parts of water plants.

In MD, look for them (and Greater Scaup) at Sandy Point State Park, Chesapeake Environmental Center, and in Cambridge on the Choptank River; in VA, watch for them at Grandview Nature Preserve. Common November–April.

Usually silent.

Greater Scaup is fairly common on open Bay waters late October–April.

Male (right) and female (left). Male is black with white forehead and nape patch (not shown) and black spot on white-and-orange bill. Female has whitish bar behind bill and white ear patch.

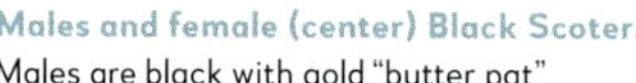

Males and female (center) Black Scoter. Males are black with gold "butter pat" atop bill. Female has pale head with contrasting blackish crown and hindneck.

Male White-winged Scoter. White wing patches (most easily seen in flight) and white eye crescent. Long face with orange bill tip.

Female White-winged Scoter. White wing patches (most easily seen in flight). Otherwise as dark as male, but with twin round, distinct head spots.

SURF SCOTER

Melanitta perspicillata Length: 20" / Wingspan: 30"

Dark and fast, scoters travel in linear flocks strung out just above rough, salty waters. If you are lucky enough to see a resting scoter flock, check it carefully because scoter species often mingle.

Dives deep in open Bay waters, propelled by both wings and feet, swallowing mussels and other mollusks whole. Also eats fish spawn and other aquatic prey.

Watch for them at Grandview Nature Preserve, Fort Monroe, and Windmill Point, VA, and at Point Lookout State Park and Great Marsh Park in Cambridge, MD. Fairly common, especially on lower half of Bay, October–April.

Usually silent.

Often seen with Black Scoter and sometimes the less-common White-winged.

Nonbreeding male. Mostly white head with black head spot, black chest, and long black tail.

Nonbreeding female. Much white but with blackish head spot and brown chest and back. Short bill.

LONG-TAILED DUCK

Clangula hyemalis Length: 16.5"/ Wingspan: 28"

This easy-to-identify "sea duck" thrills Bay-area birders late fall through winter. While on the Bay, both male and female have white heads with distinctive large dark spots. The male's elegant long tail makes it the "pintail of sea ducks." In breeding season, both male and female have dark heads punctuated with white.

Open Bay waters. Uses both wings and feet to dive for mollusks, crustaceans, and sometimes fish.

Look for them at Cambridge (Great Marsh Park and Oakley Street), Thomas Point Park, and North Beach and Chesapeake Beach, MD, and at Grandview Nature Preserve and Fort Monroe, VA. Fairly common November–March.

Male makes yodel-like *uh-uh-aaauwek*. Females grunt and quack.

Mainly white plumage, face spots, and male's long tail make identification easy.

Male.
All white below. Most of head behind eye is also white.

Female and immature.
Dark, rounded head with large white horizontal oval in center. Small bill and body.

BUFFLEHEAD

Bucephala albeola Length: 13.5" / Wingspan: 21"

This fetching bird is one of North America's smallest waterfowl species and among the Bay's most common diving ducks. The male's gleaming white head patch and body make identification easy, even from far away.

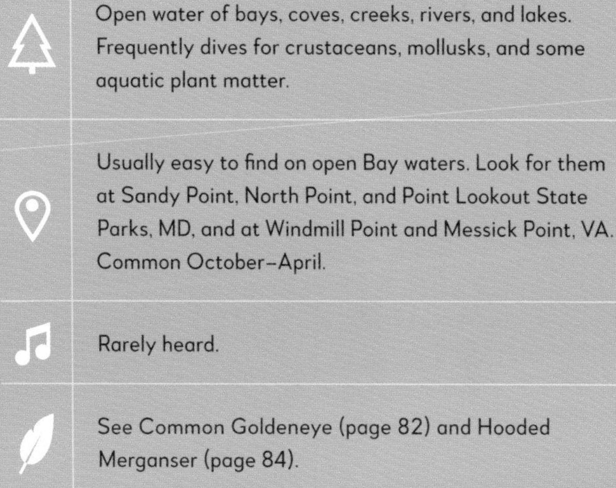

Open water of bays, coves, creeks, rivers, and lakes. Frequently dives for crustaceans, mollusks, and some aquatic plant matter.

Usually easy to find on open Bay waters. Look for them at Sandy Point, North Point, and Point Lookout State Parks, MD, and at Windmill Point and Messick Point, VA. Common October–April.

Rarely heard.

See Common Goldeneye (page 82) and Hooded Merganser (page 84).

Male.
White below, with white slashes fringing otherwise black back. Round spot between yellow eye and dark bill. In certain light, head shows green tinge.

Female.
Chocolate-brown rounded head with yellow eye and bill tip.

COMMON GOLDENEYE

Bucephala clangula Length: 18.5" / Wingspan: 26"

Usually seen well out on open water, this handsome round-headed duck is often not as plentiful as many other species wintering on the Bay. In fact, this hardy bird winters in larger numbers further north, from Long Island into Canada's Maritimes. Males are distinctive, with a large round spot behind the bill and diagonal white slashes decorating the back. Both sexes have piercing yellow eyes.

Found in small flocks on open Bay and river waters. Dives to feed on mollusks, crustaceans, fish, marine worms, and some plant matter.

Look for them at Eastern Neck National Wildlife Refuge and Sandy Point and Point Lookout State Parks, MD, and at Grandview Nature Preserve, VA. Fairly common November–March.

Harsh *eh...eh!*

See Bufflehead (page 80).

Males with crests raised. Sail-like black head with large white patch resembling inverted comma.

Female with crest raised. Head dark except for in back, where it is buff orange and shaggy. Thin merganser bill.

HOODED MERGANSER

Lophodytes cucullatus Length: 18" / Wingspan: 24"

Dazzling drakes have "expressive" crests that change their head shape. With crests lowered, males look hammer-headed, their white head patches compressed to a wedge. When a male's crest is raised, the head shape resembles a rounded sail and the white patch expands to a big, bold inverted comma.

Swamps, ponds, marsh edges, lakes, and other calm waters. Dives for fish, crayfish, crabs, and a wide variety of aquatic insects. Nests in tree cavities and Wood Duck boxes.

Look for them at Blackwater and Eastern Neck National Wildlife Refuges, Chesapeake Bay Environmental Center, and North Point State Park, MD, and at Messick Point and the ponds and coves of Newport News and Norfolk, VA. Common October–March; scarce but increasing as a nesting bird.

Male's odd courtship call is muffled yet emphatic *burrf-bvvvvrrrr*. Female utters agitated croak note, often while in flight.

See Red-breasted Merganser (page 86) and Wood Duck (page 56).

Breeding male (top) and female (bottom).
Male has dark head, white neck band and rust chest. Female has pale gold head. Both have jagged backswept crests (not visible in flight) and thin, red, pointed bills.

Breeding male (left) and female (right) Common Merganser.
Male is white below, including chest, with sharply contrasting dark green head. Lacks crest. Female has rich orange-rust head with contrasting white throat and less pronounced crest than Red-breasted.

RED-BREASTED MERGANSER

Mergus serrator Length: 23" / Wingspan: 30"

During frequent dives, this large duck grabs aquatic animals with its narrow, serrated "sawbill." This showy bird is seen on open, even choppy waters, especially those of the saltier Lower Bay.

Salty and brackish open waters of the Bay and coast. Eats a wide variety of small fish, and also crustaceans and some marine worms.

Look for them at Eastern Neck National Wildlife Refuge, Point Lookout State Park, and Elms Beach Park, MD, and at Hughlett Point Natural Area Preserve, Kiptopeke and First Landing State Parks, and Fort Monroe, VA. Fairly common, especially on Lower Bay, November–early May.

Female makes *grek grek* call.

Similar Common Merganser is more frequently seen on the Upper Bay.

Breeding male.
White cheek sharply contrasts with black cap and hindneck. Brick-red body and blue bill.

Nonbreeding male.
Contrasting black cap and white cheek. Stiff tail often cocked in both females and males.

Female and juvenile.
Dark cap and cheek line.

RUDDY DUCK

Oxyura jamaicensis Length: 15" / Wingspan: 18.5"

This compact bird stands out from the crowd by its round shape and small size and its cocked, stiff tail. It often hangs out in flocks.

Lakes, bays, and other sheltered open water. Dives for aquatic invertebrates and some plant matter, including seeds.

Look for them at Fort Monroe, VA, and at Eastern Neck National Wildlife Refuge and Sandy Point State Park, MD. Common October–April.

Seldom vocalizes.

See Bufflehead (page 80).

Breeding.
White bill with black ring. Black throat.

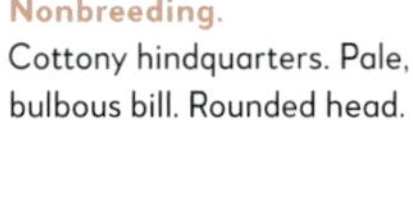

Nonbreeding.
Cottony hindquarters. Pale, bulbous bill. Rounded head.

PIED-BILLED GREBE

Podilymbus podiceps Length: 13" / Wingspan: 16"

This bird is told from ducks by its cottony hindquarters, elevated lower back, and chubby, conical bill. A bold black band rings its bill late winter through summer.

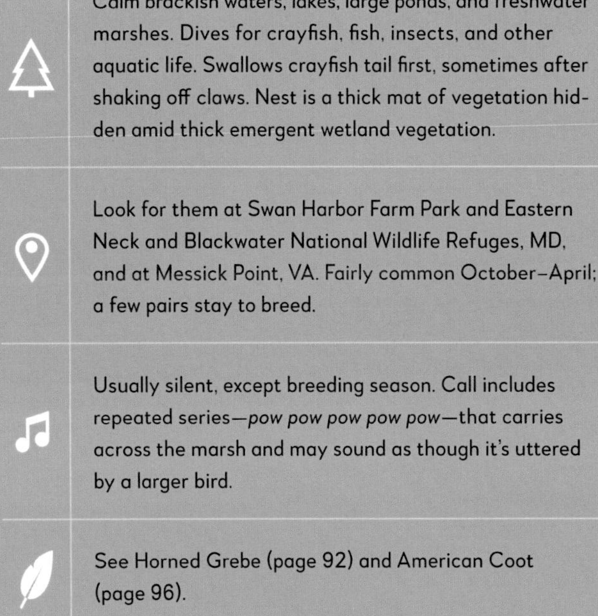

Calm brackish waters, lakes, large ponds, and freshwater marshes. Dives for crayfish, fish, insects, and other aquatic life. Swallows crayfish tail first, sometimes after shaking off claws. Nest is a thick mat of vegetation hidden amid thick emergent wetland vegetation.

Look for them at Swan Harbor Farm Park and Eastern Neck and Blackwater National Wildlife Refuges, MD, and at Messick Point, VA. Fairly common October–April; a few pairs stay to breed.

Usually silent, except breeding season. Call includes repeated series—*pow pow pow pow pow*—that carries across the marsh and may sound as though it's uttered by a larger bird.

See Horned Grebe (page 92) and American Coot (page 96).

Breeding.
Shaggy gold ear patch contrasts with otherwise black face. Rusty neck.

Nonbreeding.
Mostly white head with contrasting black cap and blackish back of neck.

Nonbreeding Eared Grebe.
Dark on head often extends over entire cheek. Front of head may appear peaked. Bill shape more thornlike thanks to upswept lower mandible.

Nonbreeding Red-necked Grebe.
Resembles a small loon in overall shape. Long, yellowish bill. Contrasting whitish from throat to behind "ear."

HORNED GREBE

Podiceps auritus Length: 14" / Wingspan: 18"

This elegant little diving bird undergoes a major transformation in March and April. As it heads north to breeding areas, it molts from "basic" dark ash and white plumage to gaudy rust, black, and yellow breeding plumage. It returns to the Bay in fall in its bicolored basic plumage.

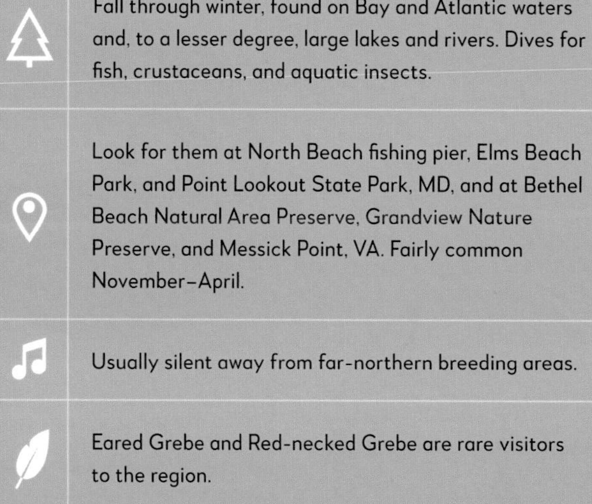

Fall through winter, found on Bay and Atlantic waters and, to a lesser degree, large lakes and rivers. Dives for fish, crustaceans, and aquatic insects.

Look for them at North Beach fishing pier, Elms Beach Park, and Point Lookout State Park, MD, and at Bethel Beach Natural Area Preserve, Grandview Nature Preserve, and Messick Point, VA. Fairly common November–April.

Usually silent away from far-northern breeding areas.

Eared Grebe and Red-necked Grebe are rare visitors to the region.

Breeding.
Dark head with necklace of vertical white bars. White chest. Checkerboard back.

Nonbreeding.
Two-toned thick neck—dark behind, light in front with thin whitish collar wedge. Thick gray dagger bill, held horizontal.

Nonbreeding Red-throated Loon.
Thin bill held up at slight angle. Neater head and neck pattern, dark gray on crown and in trim line down hindneck. (Immature birds not as distinctive, but note less heavy build and thinner bill than Common.)

COMMON LOON

Gavia immer Length: 32" / Wingspan: 46"

Each spring, Common Loons pass through the Bay region decked out in dazzling breeding plumage, en route to northern nesting lakes. During winter on the Bay, they wear toned-down plumage, with the dark gray neck usually showing a white collar wedge. Loons sit lower in the water than do most ducks, and they have long necks and dagger-like bills.

Found on Bay and Atlantic waters fall through early spring; also on some large lakes and rivers, especially during migration. Dives primarily for schooling and bottom fish, but also for crustaceans.

Look for them at Point Lookout State Park and North Beach fishing pier, MD, and at Windmill Point, Kiptopeke State Park, and Fort Monroe, VA. October–early May; fairly common on Lower Bay and uncommon on Upper Bay.

Wavering tremolo call (like a fast *wah-ha-weeheeo*) sometimes heard.

November–April, Red-throated Loon is fairly common where the Bay meets the Atlantic, but is scarce on the rest of the Bay. (Common off Atlantic beaches.)

Adult.
Virtually all blackish, with striking white bill touched with black. Lobed feet.

Breeding adult Common Gallinule.
Red forehead and bill, yellow bill tip. White blaze across sides.

AMERICAN COOT

Fulica americana

Length: 15.5" / Wingspan: 24"

This white-billed, slate-colored bird may look and act like a duck, but it's actually a member of the rail family. It formerly wintered on the Upper Bay in large numbers, but has declined there following the retreat of submerged aquatic vegetation.

Found in wetlands, coves, and lakes, feeding on aquatic plants. Submerges, picks at the surface, or walks the water's edge. Also eats a wide variety of small aquatic creatures. Nest is a floating heap of dead plant matter attached to tall, live marsh vegetation.

Look for them at Beaverdam Park and Waterford Pointe, VA, and at Perryville Community Park and Swan Harbor Farm Park, MD. Uncommon October–April; rare breeder in region.

Quick, raspy *perk*, often repeated. Female's vocalizations are noticeably lower pitched.

In the Bay region, Common Gallinule is a scarce breeder and visitor.

Adult.
Dark gray-and-white barring on flanks. Grayish face with long orange bill. Tan-olive chest and belly.

Adult King Rail.
Size and shape as in Clapper, but more richly colored, with black-and-white flanks and orange neck to belly.

Adult Virginia Rail.
Much smaller and shorter necked, with contrasting gray face and orangey breast and belly.

Adult Sora.
Short yellow bill contrasts with black face and throat. Much of head and breast bluish.

CLAPPER RAIL

Rallus crepitans Length: 14.5" / Wingspan: 19"

Rails are hard to spot, but sometimes the Clapper Rail surprises, foraging out in the open at low tide, resembling a long-billed, grayish chicken patrolling the marsh edge.

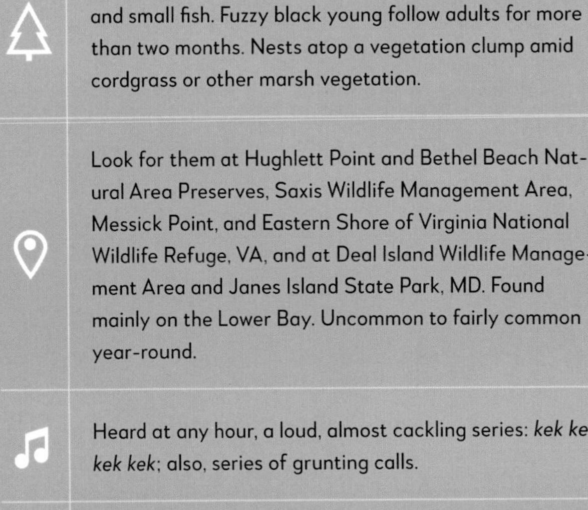

Brackish and salt marshes. Eats crustaceans, insects, and small fish. Fuzzy black young follow adults for more than two months. Nests atop a vegetation clump amid cordgrass or other marsh vegetation.

Look for them at Hughlett Point and Bethel Beach Natural Area Preserves, Saxis Wildlife Management Area, Messick Point, and Eastern Shore of Virginia National Wildlife Refuge, VA, and at Deal Island Wildlife Management Area and Janes Island State Park, MD. Found mainly on the Lower Bay. Uncommon to fairly common year-round.

Heard at any hour, a loud, almost cackling series: *kek kek kek kek*; also, series of grunting calls.

King Rail (fresh water as well as brackish) and smaller Virginia Rail and Sora.

Displaying male. Bronzy tail and tail band. Blue face with pointed or dangling "snood" and reddish throat. Colorful metallic sheen to body feathers.

Female with poults. Barred wings and bronzy tail and tail band. Bluish head less colorful than in male. Lacks snood.

WILD TURKEY

Meleagris gallopavo Length: 46" / Wingspan: 64" (females smaller)

Many years of restoration efforts brought this distinctly North American game bird back to the Bay region.

Forages on the ground, eating waste grain, insects, and the fallen nuts of oak, hickory, and beech. Roosts in trees. Nest is a hollow in the ground, littered with leaves and grasses. Sometimes seen in large flocks.

Look for them in farm fields bordering woodland and at Eastern Neck and Blackwater National Wildlife Refuges, MD, and at Hughlett Point Natural Area Preserve, VA. Fairly common year-round, but recent declines in some areas.

Males emit well-known gobbling calls; also, *chuk* and whine given by female.

Domesticated turkeys belong to the same species but are usually white or much lighter in color. If dark, they may have whitish tail bands.

Adult.
Black head and back. Bright red bill. All white below. Thick, long pale legs.

Adult Black-necked Stilt.
Most of neck white, as is spot above eye. Long, thin black bill. Very long and thin, candy-pink legs.

AMERICAN OYSTERCATCHER

Haematopus palliatus Length: 17" / Wingspan: 30"

With its bold coloration and boisterous ways, this large shorebird stands out on shellfish beds and flats of the Lower Bay. The region's population grew after the birds began nesting in secluded saltmarsh and island habitats, in addition to beach and dune zones. This bird is among the Bay's earliest nesters, courting in March and laying eggs in April.

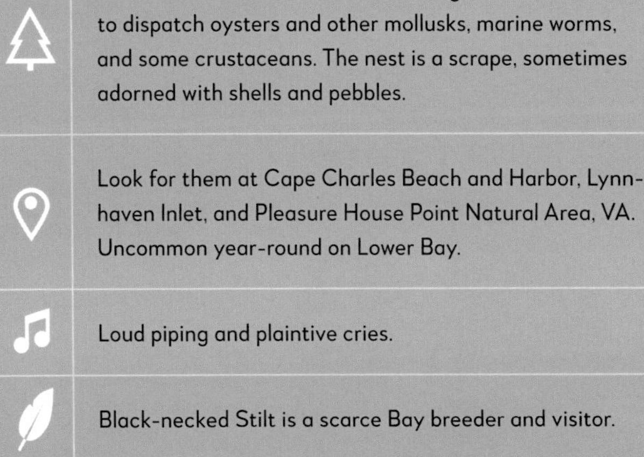

Feeds at shellfish beds and flats, using its chisel-like bill to dispatch oysters and other mollusks, marine worms, and some crustaceans. The nest is a scrape, sometimes adorned with shells and pebbles.

Look for them at Cape Charles Beach and Harbor, Lynnhaven Inlet, and Pleasure House Point Natural Area, VA. Uncommon year-round on Lower Bay.

Loud piping and plaintive cries.

Black-necked Stilt is a scarce Bay breeder and visitor.

Breeding adult.
Snow-white back scalloped in black. Jet-black face to belly.

Nonbreeding adult.
Thick bill and stocky neck. Grayish back and smudgy breast. In flight, watch for black "wingpits."

Nonbreeding adult American Golden-Plover.
Smaller head and thinner, shorter bill.

BLACK-BELLIED PLOVER

Pluvialis squatarola Length: 11.5" / Wingspan: 29"

Although much more common along the Atlantic Coast, this chunky, thick-billed Arctic nester migrates over the Bay and pops up in many spots each year. Its plaintive flight call and black "wingpits" help identify it. In spring, this bird is striking—snow-white with black scaling above and ink-black below.

Found on mudflats, wet grassy fields, shellfish beds, and shoreline, where it feeds on marine worms, mollusks, and crustaceans.

Most frequent on the Lower Bay. Look for them at Grandview Nature Preserve, Bethel Beach Natural Area Preserve, and Machicomoco State Park, VA. Usually seen alone or in small flocks. Fairly common August–November and May; uncommon in winter.

Sad-sounding *peeeoeeet*, dipping then rising.

American Golden-Plover is a scarce migrant late August–October, often in drier, grassy areas, although both species sometimes occur together.

Adult.
Two black chest bands. For a plover, has a long bill, which is all dark.

Breeding adult Semipalmated Plover.
Single dark brown chest band. Short orange-and-black bill. Orange legs. (Bill pattern and forehead are less distinct in fall and winter.)

KILLDEER

Charadrius vociferus Length: 10.5" / Wingspan: 24"

This noisy, double-banded plover is a fixture in habitats both wet and dry across the Bay region, belting out its namesake kill-DEE call day or night.

Open areas, including wetlands, farm fields, gravelly lots, golf courses, and airports. Nest is a scrape on open ground, sometimes lined with debris like pebbles. Eats insects, including beetles and grasshoppers, and other invertebrates.

Watch for them in wetlands and farm fields at Blackwater National Wildlife Refuge, MD; at Messick Point, Windmill Point, and Fort Monroe, VA; and in many agricultural areas. Some nest on flat, gravelly rooftops. Common much of year, though uncommon in winter along Upper Bay.

Ringing *kill-dee* call is hard to miss, given during courtship and at other times. *Key-dee-dee* call also frequently heard from birds on alert.

Semipalmated Plover is a common migrant, especially on the Lower Bay, where it is scarce in winter.

Nonbreeding adult. Mid-sized, brownish gray above, with long, droop-tipped bill. This individual has vestiges of breeding plumage—the blackish on belly and rusty back feathers.

Short-billed Dowitcher. Longer, totally straight bill. Buffy below (gray in winter) with spotty sides of neck. (Long-billed Dowitcher, not shown, is very similar but generally less common; has barred sides of neck and sometimes visibly longer bill.)

DUNLIN

Calidris alpina

Length: 8.5" / Wingspan: 17"

This mid-sized, droop-billed shorebird is one of the most common wintering sandpipers on the Bay. Drably colored fall through March, the Dunlin transforms into a rusty-backed, black-bellied beauty as it heads north to tundra nesting grounds in April and May.

Feeds on mudflats, beaches, and sometimes flooded fields, walking along and dipping its bill to snatch worms, small mollusks, crustaceans, and insects.

Look for them at Blackwater National Wildlife Refuge, MD, and at Hughlett Point and Bethel Beach Natural Area Preserves and Messick Point, VA. Common on Lower Bay, uncommon on Upper Bay, October–May.

Call sharp, burry *buff* or *beev*.

Although more numerous along the Atlantic Coast, Short-billed and Long-billed Dowitchers also pass through the Lower Bay during migration. The much smaller Western Sandpiper is an uncommon late-summer migrant (see photo in Least Sandpiper entry, page 110).

Juvenile.
Pale yellow legs. In all plumages, this species is brown backed with streaky, brown-washed breast and pale yellow legs. Juveniles have rusty scalloping on back.

Semipalmated Sandpiper.
Grayer on back, with spare, light breast streaking. Black legs and straight bill.

Western Sandpiper.
Spring to summer, some rust color on back and head. Small spots below. Droop-tipped bill. Black legs.

White-rumped Sandpiper.
Larger. Wingtips at rest extend beyond the tail. Streaked flanks. All-white rump in flight (the region's other peeps have dark bar running through center of rump).

LEAST SANDPIPER

Calidris minutilla Length: 6" / Wingspan: 13"

This sparrow-sized shorebird is the smallest and brownest of the nondescript "peeps," and sports pale yellow legs. It frequents slightly drier mud than its cousins, often foraging a bit farther from water.

Found on mudflats, shorelines, and flooded fields, where it pecks and probes for tiny invertebrates. Usually in flocks, often mixed with other peeps and Semipalmated Plovers.

Look for them at North Beach, Blackwater National Wildlife Refuge, and Point Lookout State Park, MD, and at Hughlett Point and Bethel Beach Natural Area Preserves and First Landing State Park, VA. Fairly common April–May and July–September. Scarce in winter.

Call is a brief, rising trill.

Semipalmated Sandpiper is another frequently seen peep; Western and White-rumped Sandpipers are less numerous. Note: Plumage on peep species varies by age and season, and identification is often challenging.

Adult.
Striped back and face. Heavy barring below. Very long, straight bill and large, dark eye.

Adult American Woodcock (with chick).
Unmarked and pale orange below. Large, dark eye and very long, straight bill. Black squares on top of head.

WILSON'S SNIPE

Gallinago delicata Length: 10.5" / Wingspan: 18"

Birders often stumble upon this well-camouflaged bird, which suddenly bolts into zigzag flight. The snipe's set-back eyes provide an expansive field of vision, and its stripy plumage provides excellent camouflage.

Found in marshes and flooded fields, where it probes mud and shallows for insect larvae, worms, crustaceans, and mollusks. Found singly or in small flocks.

Look for them at Blackwater National Wildlife Refuge, North Beach, and Chesapeake Beach, MD, and at Saxis Wildlife Management Area, VA. Uncommon October–early May.

Loud, raspy *korek!* accompanies a flushed bird's sudden takeoff and zigzag flight.

American Woodcock, a nocturnal "landpiper" found in wet forests near grassy areas, is a declining breeder, mostly seen when it displays at dusk and dawn February to April. Some winter.

Breeding adult.
Spotted below. Dark brown above. Orange bill. White shoulder crescent.

Nonbreeding adult.
Solid dark brown back. White shoulder crescent. Brown breast smudge.

Solitary Sandpiper.
Small round white spots on dark brown back. White eyering. Straight, dark bill.

SPOTTED SANDPIPER

Actitis macularius

Length: 7.5" / Wingspan: 15"

This bird stands out from the shorebird crowd thanks to its tail-pumping habit, lack of streaks, and spotted breast in breeding plumage. While seen at shorelines, this bird and the Solitary Sandpiper also show up at streams and creeks.

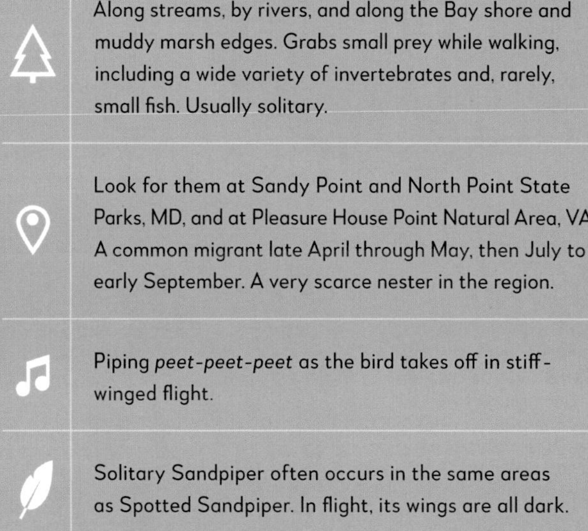

Along streams, by rivers, and along the Bay shore and muddy marsh edges. Grabs small prey while walking, including a wide variety of invertebrates and, rarely, small fish. Usually solitary.

Look for them at Sandy Point and North Point State Parks, MD, and at Pleasure House Point Natural Area, VA. A common migrant late April through May, then July to early September. A very scarce nester in the region.

Piping *peet-peet-peet* as the bird takes off in stiff-winged flight.

Solitary Sandpiper often occurs in the same areas as Spotted Sandpiper. In flight, its wings are all dark.

Adult Greater Yellowlegs (top) with adult Lesser Yellowlegs (bottom). Greater noticeably larger than Lesser and has bill longer than head length that is often slightly upswept. Lesser bill straight, roughly head length. Both species have bold yellow legs.

Adult Willet in flight. Bold black-and-white wing pattern. Large with heavy, long, straight bill. Dull bluish legs. (Yellowlegs have all-dark wings and yellow legs.)

GREATER YELLOWLEGS

Tringa melanoleuca Length: 14" / Wingspan: 28"

This large, leggy sandpiper forages in deeper water than many others, wading up to its belly on striking yellow legs and sometimes even swimming.

Feeds in shallows, at edges of wetlands, and in flooded fields. Lunges for small fish and invertebrates; also captures prey by sweeping its bill back and forth in water.

Look for them at Eastern Neck and Blackwater National Wildlife Refuges, MD, and at the Eastern Shore of Virginia National Wildlife Refuge, Messick Point, and Grandview Nature Preserve, VA. Common migrant April–May and July–October; in winter, scarce on Upper Bay and fairly common on Lower Bay.

Call a piping *tew tew tew* or *tew tew tew tew*.

Lesser Yellowlegs is a common migrant; larger Willet is fairly common year-round on Lower Bay saltmarsh mudflats and beaches.

Breeding adult.
All-black head and thin black bill. Light gray back.

Nonbreeding adult.
White head with black ear spot and thin black bill. In flight, white primary feathers stand out on otherwise light gray wings.

BONAPARTE'S GULL

Chroicocephalus philadelphia Length: 13.5" / Wingspan: 33"

Small and graceful, this gull can be easily mistaken for a tern. Usually seen in white-headed "basic" or nonbreeding plumage on the Bay; molts into black-headed breeding "dress" in time to migrate north to interior Canada and Alaska in April.

Wheels and hovers over roiling open waters, snatching small fish and insects and other invertebrates. Unlike region's other gulls, does not feed on trash or unattended food.

Look for them especially in the mid- to Lower Bay, including at Point Lookout State Park and North Beach fishing pier, MD, and at Bethel Beach Natural Area Preserve and Fort Monroe, VA. November to early March, uncommon on Upper Bay and fairly common on Lower Bay. Common migrant mid-March through April.

Calls brief and grating—less plaintive than those of other Bay gulls.

See Forster's Tern (page 128). Black-headed and Little Gulls, not shown, are rare in region.

Breeding adult. Black head, red or reddish bill, and dark gray back. White around eye.

Nonbreeding adult. Ashy smudges on head. Mostly black bill. Dark gray back. Black legs.

LAUGHING GULL

Leucophaeus atricilla Length: 16.5" / Wingspan: 40"

This familiar beach bird is usually the only black-headed gull present in summer. October to March, the head is whitish with some dark gray smudging. Laughing Gulls forage widely but nest locally in marshes.

Found along shorelines, at beaches, and in farm fields and marshes, where it walks, hovers, and dives to snatch insects, worms, crustaceans, fish, leftovers, and trash. Nest can be a hollow in a shallow mat of marsh grass and sticks, or just a scrape. Nests in colonies, usually on saltmarsh islands.

Look for them at Sandy Point and Point Lookout State Parks, MD, and at First Landing State Park, Lynnhaven Inlet, and Fort Monroe, VA. Common April–November; in region, nests mostly in VA. Scarce in winter.

Named for laughing call, which starts with chuckles and ends in long guffaws.

See Bonaparte's Gull (page 118).

Nonbreeding adult.
Yellow legs and yellow bill with black ring. Light gray back. Some smudgy streaking on head and neck. (In breeding plumage, head is clean white.)

First winter.
Pinkish bill with black tip. Light-colored but with dark scalloping on sides and mottling at wing edges. Blackish primaries and secondaries. Dark tail band easily seen in flight.

RING-BILLED GULL

Larus delawarensis Length: 17.5" / Wingspan: 48"

Fall through winter, the "ringbill" is the Bay's most common gull. Although its scientific name declares it the "Delaware Gull," this adaptable bird actually breeds much farther north.

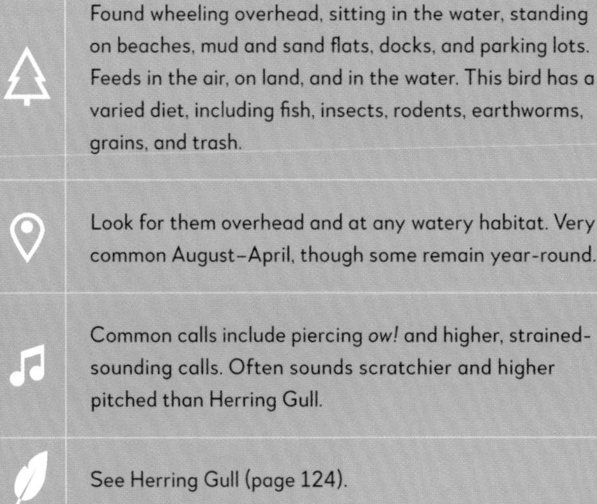

Found wheeling overhead, sitting in the water, standing on beaches, mud and sand flats, docks, and parking lots. Feeds in the air, on land, and in the water. This bird has a varied diet, including fish, insects, rodents, earthworms, grains, and trash.

Look for them overhead and at any watery habitat. Very common August–April, though some remain year-round.

Common calls include piercing *ow!* and higher, strained-sounding calls. Often sounds scratchier and higher pitched than Herring Gull.

See Herring Gull (page 124).

Nonbreeding adult.
Pink legs. Light gray back. Smudgy streaks on much of head. Sturdy yellow bill with pink spot. (Head clean white in breeding plumage.)

First winter.
All dark brown body, with black on much of upper tail and outer primary flight feathers. Pale head with blackish bill.

HERRING GULL

Larus argentatus Length: 25" / Wingspan: 58"

Though often shrugged off as a common bird, this species almost vanished along the East Coast due to market hunting of adults and eggs in the 1800s. The Migratory Bird Treaty Act helped this resilient bird march back from the brink, along with many other species.

Usually on or close to water, where it feeds on a wide variety of foods, including fish, starfish, worms, shellfish, and trash. A pair makes a bowl-shaped nest of dead marsh grasses, washed-up debris, and feathers. Commonly mingles with other gull species.

Look for them at jetties and beaches, in marshes, and on and over Bay waters. Increasing as a breeding species. Common year-round.

Common calls include clear and familiar *gulla gulla gulla clear clear clear clear clear.*

See Ring-billed Gull (page 122).

Adult.
Virtually all-white head with heavy yellow bill with pink spot. Pink legs. Very dark back.

First winter.
Very large gull with back checkered with blackish and white. Heavy black bill. White head.

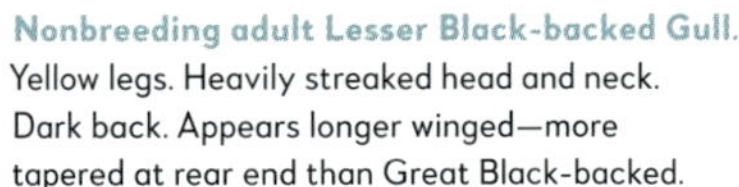

Nonbreeding adult Lesser Black-backed Gull.
Yellow legs. Heavily streaked head and neck. Dark back. Appears longer winged—more tapered at rear end than Great Black-backed. (All-white head when breeding.)

First winter Lesser Black-backed Gull.
Dark back often appears less checkered and overall a bit darker than in Great. Whitish head contrasts with heavy grayish streaking on underparts. Black bill.

GREAT BLACK-BACKED GULL

Larus marinus Length: 30" / Wingspan: 65"

North America's largest gull muscles its way into a variety of feeding opportunities. As do Herring Gulls, Great Black-backed Gulls raid other seabirds' nests and drop shellfish, eggs, and chicks onto hard surfaces before eating them. They dine on trash as well, though seldom while feeding their young.

On and over open water. Rests on beaches, mudflats, jetties, bridge railings, and light poles. Feeds on marine life, insects, mammals, eggs, birds, carrion, and trash. Nest is a bowl scraped into mud, grasses, or sand, made with vegetation and some other debris gathered nearby.

Look for them at Sandy Point State Park, on the Route 50 Bay Bridge, and in Cambridge, MD, and at Bethel Beach Natural Area Preserve, Lynnhaven Inlet, and Fort Monroe, VA. Common year-round.

Utters deeper, more hollow-sounding calls than do other local gulls.

Though generally uncommon, Lesser Black-backed Gull is an increasingly frequent Bay visitor.

Breeding adult.
All-white underparts and whitish primaries (outer flight feathers) contrast with light gray back. Black cap and orange bill with black tip.

Nonbreeding adult.
Black mask framed by white crown and nape. Much whitish on wings (dark gray on wingtips). All-black bill.

Breeding adult Common Tern.
Light gray underparts and back. Whitish head with black cap and dark red bill.

Breeding adult Least Tern.
Smaller than other terns, with short tail and faster wingbeats. White forehead stands out from otherwise black cap. Yellow bill.

FORSTER'S TERN

Sterna forsteri Length: 14" / Wingspan: 31"

Mostly gleaming white, this buoyant seabird is the Upper Bay's most commonly seen tern. In most plumages, a distinctive black ear patch clinches identification. March–August, though, adults have a sleek black cap, closely resembling the Common Tern.

Found in marshes and over rivers and the Bay, diving for small fish. Nests in marshes, often on mats of vegetation. On the Bay, nesting birds face an uncertain future due to climate-related coastline change and loss of nesting islands.

Look for them at Blackwater National Wildlife Refuge and Point Lookout State Park, MD, and at Messick Point and Bethel Beach Natural Area Preserve, VA. Common April–November; the only expected tern in winter (uncommon).

Slightly trilling yet clear, almost gull-like *keeerr*. Also, buzzy *prrrt*.

Common and Least Terns nest in some areas and wander widely, but they are absent late fall through winter. See also Royal Tern (page 130).

Breeding adult.
Short, ragged crest and all-orange-reddish bill. Wings more slender than Caspian's, and underwing virtually all white.

Nonbreeding adult.
White forehead, orange bill. At rest, shows short, ragged crest.

Breeding adult Caspian Tern.
Larger with thicker build than Royal. Wingtips dark underneath. Black cap and thick red bill. Tail notched, not deeply forked as in Royal.

Nonbreeding adult Caspian Tern.
Same as breeding, except forehead heavily streaked (not white as in nonbreeding Royal).

ROYAL TERN

Thalasseus maximus Length: 20" / Wingspan: 41"

Starting in April, 5000 to 6000 pairs of this large tern return to nest at Fort Wool in Hampton, Virginia, at the bottom of the Bay. This largest Bay tern colony was relocated in 2020 due to construction on the Hampton Roads bridge–tunnel complex.

Dives for fish in salty, open Bay waters; sometimes snatches small crabs. The nest is a scrape in sand or gravel, usually on islands safe from mammalian predators. Nests in colonies.

Look for them at Messick Point, Windmill Point, Lynnhaven Inlet, and Fort Monroe, VA, which is near the Hampton colony. Common on the Lower Bay April–November; after nesting, wanders the Upper Bay as well from July to November.

Two-syllable call: *kar-rick*.

Caspian Tern is a fairly common Bay migrant April to early May and late July to early October. Sandwich Terns, Gull-billed Terns, and Black Skimmers (not shown) also nest at Fort Wool, as do Common Terns; they forage across the Lower Bay as well.

Adult.
Gleaming white with black wingtips and pale yellow head. Whitish cone-like bill. Note: First-year birds are all dark except for white on rump and dinginess on belly and underwings. Older immatures show more of a mix of whitish and dark.

Adult Brown Booby.
Dark brown with sharply contrasting white belly, undertail, and inner parts of underwing. Yellow bill and feet.

NORTHERN GANNET

Morus bassanus Length: 37" / Wingspan: 72"

After nesting in huge colonies off Canada's Atlantic Coast, this northern booby winters along the entire East Coast and into the Gulf of Mexico. Immaculate white adults with jet-black wingtips can be seen from quite a distance. Their flight is direct, with deep wing strokes. It takes a gannet four years to attain gleaming adult plumage.

Plunges dart-like for fish, hitting the water at speeds over 60 miles per hour and submerging 15 or more feet below the water's surface. Often descends further, using wings and feet, pursuing prey to 50 feet or more.

Look for them at Point Lookout State Park and North Beach, MD, and at Kiptopeke State Park fishing pier, Bethel Beach Natural Area Preserve, Windmill Point, and Fort Monroe, VA. A fairly common migrant to the Lower Bay, November–April.

Silent away from northern nesting colonies.

Brown Booby has become a rare but rather regular Bay visitor, with sightings July–December.

Nonbreeding adult. All dark except for orange pouch and lores. (Green eye not often seen unless close.)

Juvenile. Orange pouch, bill, and lores. Light tan with whitish from throat to dark belly.

Nonbreeding adult Great Cormorant. Squarish head, thick bill, and two-toned throat. Dark lores.

Juvenile Great Cormorant. Squarish head, thick bill. Dark neck and breast contrast with whitish belly.

DOUBLE-CRESTED CORMORANT

Nannopterum auritum Length: 33" / Wingspan: 52"

Rather goose-like in flight and loon-like while swimming, this glossy black bird propels itself underwater with strong webbed feet, hunting schooling and bottom-feeding fish by sight and feel.

Found in open shallow waters and over the Bay in small to large flocks. Dives for fish and some aquatic invertebrates. Nest is a bulky, globular collection of sticks, seaweed, and collected debris placed on the ground, in trees or shrubs, or on a structure. Nests in colonies.

Look for them across the region, swimming or standing by the water's edge, often holding their wings out to dry. Common year-round. A localized breeder, in scattered colonies.

Usually silent away from colonies, but sometimes grunts.

Great Cormorant is a scarce winter visitor to the Bay.

Breeding adult.
Brown hindneck, blackish pouch, and yellow on crown. Dark brown body and gray back. (Nonbreeding birds have white hindnecks and little yellow on head.)

Juvenile.
Brown with contrasting whitish belly.

Nonbreeding adult American White Pelican.
All white except for black flight feathers and bright orange bill.

BROWN PELICAN

Pelecanus occidentalis Length: 51" / Wingspan: 79"

While diving for fish, the Brown Pelican fills its throat pouch with up to 2.5 gallons of water, which drains out, leaving only its meal. Conservation measures and bans on harmful pesticides enabled this once-rare bird to rebound and expand its breeding range northward to the Lower Bay.

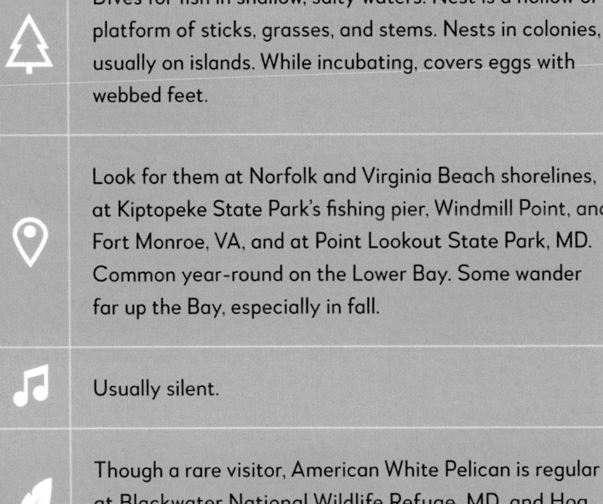

Dives for fish in shallow, salty waters. Nest is a hollow or platform of sticks, grasses, and stems. Nests in colonies, usually on islands. While incubating, covers eggs with webbed feet.

Look for them at Norfolk and Virginia Beach shorelines, at Kiptopeke State Park's fishing pier, Windmill Point, and Fort Monroe, VA, and at Point Lookout State Park, MD. Common year-round on the Lower Bay. Some wander far up the Bay, especially in fall.

Usually silent.

Though a rare visitor, American White Pelican is regular at Blackwater National Wildlife Refuge, MD, and Hog Island Wildlife Management Area, VA.

Adult.
Hunched posture. Striking contrast between black crown and back and light gray wings and underparts. White face and head plumes.

Juvenile.
Large teardrop-like spots on back and yellowish on bill. Shorter necked and overall lighter than immature Yellow-crowned.

Adult Yellow-crowned Night Heron.
White cheek patch and pale yellow crown on otherwise black head. Dull bluish body. White head plumes.

Juvenile Yellow-crowned Night Heron.
Blackish bill and longer neck. Darker overall, with smaller back spots.

BLACK-CROWNED NIGHT HERON

Nycticorax nycticorax Length: 25" / Wingspan: 44"

Despite eye-catching plumage, this squat, medium-sized heron is easily overlooked because it mainly hunts at dawn, dusk, and night. During the day, it roosts amid the leafy cover of trees and tall shrubs, often along the water's edge.

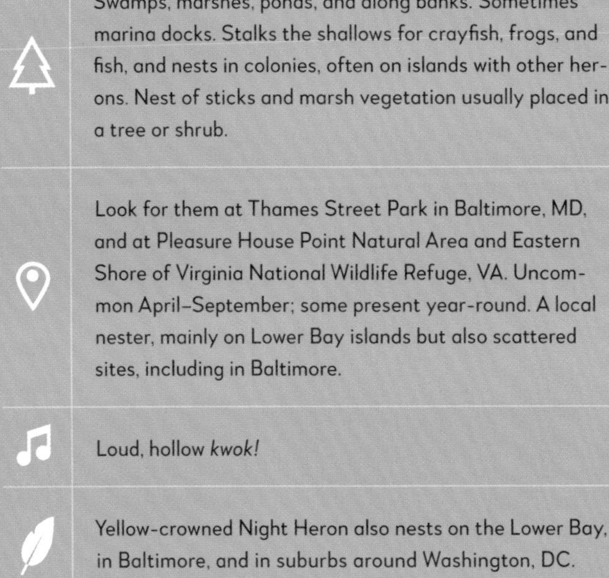

Swamps, marshes, ponds, and along banks. Sometimes marina docks. Stalks the shallows for crayfish, frogs, and fish, and nests in colonies, often on islands with other herons. Nest of sticks and marsh vegetation usually placed in a tree or shrub.

Look for them at Thames Street Park in Baltimore, MD, and at Pleasure House Point Natural Area and Eastern Shore of Virginia National Wildlife Refuge, VA. Uncommon April–September; some present year-round. A local nester, mainly on Lower Bay islands but also scattered sites, including in Baltimore.

Loud, hollow *kwok!*

Yellow-crowned Night Heron also nests on the Lower Bay, in Baltimore, and in suburbs around Washington, DC.

Adult.
Greenish back and wings with contrasting rusty neck and head. Dark cap. Short orange legs.

Juvenile.
Rust-streaked neck and dark cap. Dark wings with many light markings. Short yellow legs.

Adult Least Bittern.
Smaller than Green Heron. Mostly warm caramel color, with contrasting dark back and cap. Yellow-orange bill. In flight, flashes buffy wing patches.

GREEN HERON

Butorides virescens Length: 18" / Wingspan: 26"

This compact, reddish-necked bird is one of few tool-using birds, sometimes placing twigs or leaves on the water's surface to lure prey into striking range. It is the region's most widespread nesting heron.

Swamps, ponds, marsh edges, and areas with calm water and thick vegetation. Sits on perches in shallow water or hunkers down along banks; sometimes stalks prey, primarily fish and invertebrates. Usually a solitary nester, with stick nest at or above eye level in a small tree or large shrub.

Look for them at overgrown drainage ponds and many other wetlands including those at Eastern Neck National Wildlife Refuge, MD, and at Pleasure House Point Natural Area, VA. Common mid-April–September. Outside nesting season, usually seen alone.

Explosive *keeyoh!* that often echoes across a marsh.

Least Bittern, the area's smallest heron, is a localized nester. The American Bittern (see Page 5) is a scarce to uncommon visitor and rare breeder.

Adult.
All-yellow bill and long neck. All-black legs and feet.

Adult Snowy Egret.
Black bill and yellow lores. Black legs with yellow feet. Shaggy hindneck. (Juveniles often show yellow on the backs of legs.)

Juvenile Little Blue Heron.
Black tip to pale gray bill. Greenish-yellow legs and feet (no black).

Nonbreeding adult Western Cattle-Egret.
Much smaller and shorter necked than Great. Black legs and feet; shortish yellow bill. (In breeding plumage, buff chest, crown, and back feathers.)

GREAT EGRET

Ardea alba

Length: 39" / Wingspan: 51"

Egrets are white herons, and this is the largest. Hunted to near extinction by the early 1900s for its lacy courtship feathers (used to decorate hats), this elegant wader rebounded after conservation actions.

Marshes, swamps, inlets, and ponds. Hunts the shallows, slowly striding or waiting in ambush. Diet includes fish, frogs, snakes, crustaceans, insects, and small birds. Builds its stick nest in a tree or shrub. Nests in colonies, mostly on islands in the Lower Bay.

Look for them at Blackwater National Wildlife Refuge, MD, and at Lynnhaven Inlet and New Point Comfort Natural Area Preserve, VA, and many other wetland sites. Common much of year, but scarce on the Upper Bay in winter.

Sometimes utters growls or croaks.

Snowy Egret also occurs in the Bay area, as do Little Blue Heron (immature is all white) and Western Cattle-Egret.

Breeding Adult.
Bluish body, pale gray neck, whitish face, and black head stripe runs from behind eye and includes plumes sweeping off back of neck. This bird has bluish lores only present during breeding.

Juvenile.
Mostly gray, with blackish cap that starts at eye level.

Sandhill Crane.
Red crown; mostly gray, with bushy feathers (called a bustle) over tail. Flies with neck outstretched.

GREAT BLUE HERON

Ardea herodias

Length: 54" / Wingspan: 72"

Standing 4.5 feet tall, this is the Bay's largest and most frequently seen wading bird. Herons and egrets fly with their necks curled back, unlike other long-legged wading birds.

Found in virtually all watery habitats, standing or crouching in search of small animals including crabs, fish, frogs, small mammals, and birds. Prey captured with a whiplike strike of the neck and a jab of the daggerlike bill. Breeds in colonies, building stick nests near treetops.

Look for them at Blackwater National Wildlife Refuge and Marshy Point Nature Center, MD, and at Grandview Nature Preserve and Pleasure House Point Natural Area, VA. Common year-round.

Cranky-sounding *graaaaawp* uttered on take-off.

Little Blue Heron (adult not shown) and Tricolored Heron (not shown) also occur on Lower Bay; some wander north in summer. Sandhill Crane a rare visitor.

Adult.
All white with black wingtips. Red legs and curved red-and-black bill.

Juvenile.
Curved orange bill. Brown back, brownish neck, and white belly.

Adult Glossy Ibis.
Dark rust, except for glossy blackish wings and lower back. Grayish curved bill. Thin whitish lines above and below eye.

WHITE IBIS

Eudocimus albus Length: 24" / Wingspan: 42"

This curve-billed wader is a recent addition to the Bay's avifauna. It became a regular nester in Virginia in the early 2000s and was first confirmed nesting in Maryland in 2020. Flocks are now a regular sight on the Lower Bay, spring through fall.

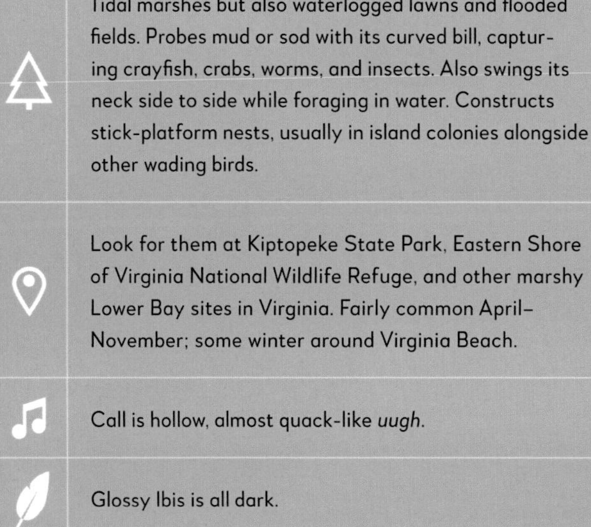

Tidal marshes but also waterlogged lawns and flooded fields. Probes mud or sod with its curved bill, capturing crayfish, crabs, worms, and insects. Also swings its neck side to side while foraging in water. Constructs stick-platform nests, usually in island colonies alongside other wading birds.

Look for them at Kiptopeke State Park, Eastern Shore of Virginia National Wildlife Refuge, and other marshy Lower Bay sites in Virginia. Fairly common April–November; some winter around Virginia Beach.

Call is hollow, almost quack-like *uugh*.

Glossy Ibis is all dark.

Adults.
Bare lead-gray head and neck.

Adult.
White wing patches and short tail. Gray head.

BLACK VULTURE

Coragyps atratus Length: 25" / Wingspan: 59"

The ultimate scrounger, this short-tailed, white-wing-patched scavenger is a familiar sight over Bay towns and outskirts. Often seen dining roadside on animal carcasses or at dumpsters.

Open habitats. Feeds on carrion, trash, and sometimes, opportunistically, eggs and young of birds and other small creatures. A retiring nester, it lays its eggs in hidden places such as tangles, abandoned structures, or hollow logs.

Soars over farmland, towns, cities, and along roadways. Roosts on tall structures and in trees. Increasingly common year-round.

Usually silent.

See Turkey Vulture (page 150).

Adult.
Bare red head with white-tipped bill. Long wings and tail. (Juveniles have dark heads but more fully feathered necks than Black Vulture.)

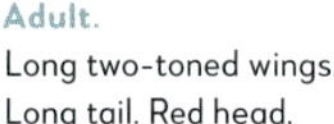

Adult.
Long two-toned wings. Long tail. Red head.

TURKEY VULTURE

Cathartes aura Length: 27" / Wingspan: 69"

This is the Bay region's most often seen raptor, soaring or gliding on two-toned wings held in a shallow V. With one of the keenest senses of smell in the bird world, it detects the scent of rotting carrion in the air column. The Black Vulture and other scavengers watch for the Turkey Vulture to descend on newly found carcasses.

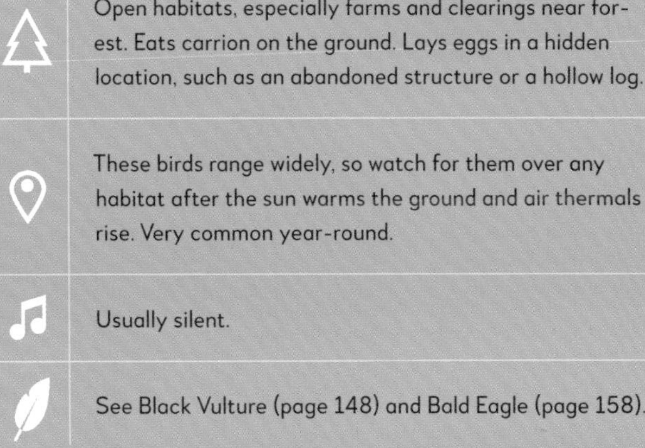

Open habitats, especially farms and clearings near forest. Eats carrion on the ground. Lays eggs in a hidden location, such as an abandoned structure or a hollow log.

These birds range widely, so watch for them over any habitat after the sun warms the ground and air thermals rise. Very common year-round.

Usually silent.

See Black Vulture (page 148) and Bald Eagle (page 158).

Adult.
Broad dark line through piercing yellow eye and dark wings and back. White on head and below, except for peppering of breast spots.

Adult.
Long, narrow gull-like wings and shallow M-like flight profile. Dark "wrist patches."

OSPREY

Pandion haliaetus Length: 23" / Wingspan: 63"

The "fish hawk" occurs on all continents except Antarctica, but the Bay is one of its largest breeding hubs, with thousands of nesting pairs. Spring through summer, you'll see channel markers, nesting platforms, water and communications towers, and even highway signs festooned with bulky, occupied nests.

Hovers then dives feetfirst for fish. Prey carried off head-first, an aerodynamic adaptation often called "packing a lunch." The nest is a bulky mass of sticks. A pair often uses the same nest year after year.

Look for them over open water anywhere along the shores of the Bay, including in Cambridge, MD, and Norfolk, VA. Very common mid-March–October. Rare in winter on Lower Bay.

Call is clipped, high-pitched *kip kip kip kip.*

See Bald Eagle (page 158).

Adult male.
Not seen as often as females and juveniles but instantly recognized by silvery-gray body and tail. White below with fine speckling. Bold white rump.

Juvenile.
Long broad wings and narrow long tail. Bold white rump patch. Buffy with some streaking below. Adult females are similar, but generally paler and more evenly streaked below.

Adult Short-eared Owl in flight.
Bulky head and shortish tail. Long but rounded wings blazed with gold. Wobbly, less direct flight than harrier.

NORTHERN HARRIER

Circus hudsonius Length: 18" / Wingspan: 43"

Nicknamed the "marsh hawk," this distinctive raptor cruises low over open marsh and fields, hovers, then pounces on prey. The long tail and white rump help identify it even from a distance.

Found in marshes, fallow fields, and meadows, the harrier hunts voles, mice, and other small mammals; also songbirds.

Look for them at Deal Island Wildlife Management Area, MD, and in VA at Saxis Wildlife Management Area and, in fall, at the hawk watch at Kiptopeke State Park. Fairly common September to mid-May; uncommon otherwise. A declining nester in Lower Bay marshes.

Sometimes utters whistles or barking calls.

In winter, Short-eared Owls may occupy the same habitats as harriers, with both sometimes seen at the same time, night shift meeting day shift.

Adult.
Gray back. Dark cap. Orange-barred breast. Long tail rounded at tip, ending with wide white band.

Juvenile.
Thin stripes throat to belly. Wide white tail tip. Brown head with indistinct pattern. In flight, Cooper's silhouette is cross-like, with longer tail and more protruding head than Sharp-shinned, which is shaped more like a T.

Adult Sharp-shinned Hawk.
Shorter, more rounded head (note dark nape) helps give it T-shaped silhouette in flight. Squared tail tip. Thin legs and small bill. In flight, has faster wingbeats on shorter wings than Cooper's.

COOPER'S HAWK

Astur cooperii Length: 16.5" / Wingspan: 31"

Long tailed with broad wings, the Cooper's Hawk specializes in hunting other birds, targeting the starling-to-pigeon size range. As with many other raptors, female Cooper's Hawks are larger than males.

Forests, at edges, and in suburbs. Hunts birds and some small mammals, remaining partially hidden then suddenly giving chase. Also drops from a high perch to capture unsuspecting prey on the ground. Stick nest is usually high in a tree, well hidden and sometimes built atop an old nest or leafy clump.

Look for them in large numbers during fall migration over Kiptopeke State Park and other hawk watch sites. Otherwise, fairly common September–May; an uncommon nester.

Seldom vocal, but young sometimes screech or call *kek kek kek kek kek kek*. Adults sometimes utter somewhat nasal calls or whistles.

Sharp-shinned Hawk is very similar. See facing page captions.

Adult.
White head and tail, and yellow bill and talons. Otherwise, all dark. Flat wing profile, in contrast to Turkey Vulture and Golden Eagle, which have shallow-V wing profiles.

Second year.
Dark head and breast. Much whitish on wings and belly (usually on tail and back as well).

Juvenile Golden Eagle.
Dark with pale gold nape. Shallow V flight profile. Adults lack bold white wing patches and base of tail seen in juveniles like this one.

BALD EAGLE

Haliaeetus leucocephalus Length: 31" / Wingspan: 80"

Our majestic national symbol is an increasingly common sight throughout the region. Pairs start nest-building as early as October and lay eggs in February. It takes up to five years for young birds to attain full adult plumage.

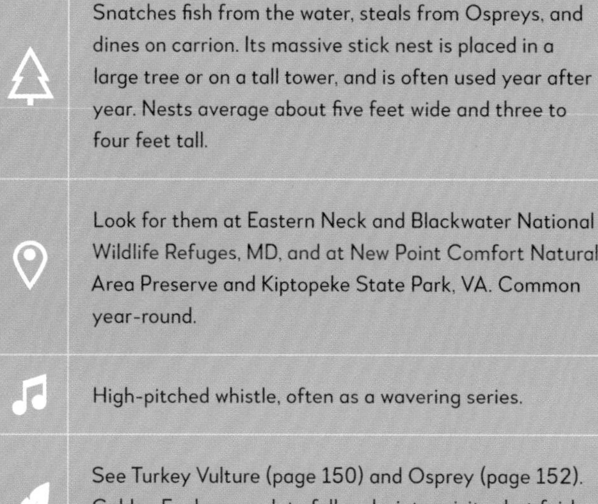

Snatches fish from the water, steals from Ospreys, and dines on carrion. Its massive stick nest is placed in a large tree or on a tall tower, and is often used year after year. Nests average about five feet wide and three to four feet tall.

Look for them at Eastern Neck and Blackwater National Wildlife Refuges, MD, and at New Point Comfort Natural Area Preserve and Kiptopeke State Park, VA. Common year-round.

High-pitched whistle, often as a wavering series.

See Turkey Vulture (page 150) and Osprey (page 152). Golden Eagle a rare late fall and winter visitor but fairly regular at Blackwater National Wildlife Refuge, MD.

Adult (from above).
Rusty shoulders. Pale arcs near wingtips. Longish dark tail with narrow white bands.

Adult.
Breast heavily barred in orange down to belly. Reddish shoulder. Checkered wings.

Broad-winged Hawk (from below).
Pale underwings outlined in black. Short tail with just one prominent white band. No pale arcs on wings.

RED-SHOULDERED HAWK

Buteo lineatus Length: 17" / Wingspan: 40"

Although considered a swamp-and-forest raptor, this orange-breasted hawk also perches on power lines and poles lining farm country. Calling pairs are often seen circling overhead.

Swamps, mixed and deciduous forest, and edges, including suburbs. From a high perch, it pounces on frogs, snakes, rodents, and other small creatures. Pairs build a bulky stick-and-leaf nest in the crotch of a tall tree, often atop an old crow nest or other nest. Breeding season starts in February.

Look for them in swamps and woods, including at Flag Ponds Nature Park, MD. Also frequently perched along roadsides. Common year-round. More common as a nester on the Western Shore.

Far-carrying *keeearr keeearr keeearr* ... Blue Jays produce a weaker imitation.

Broad-winged Hawk present mainly as a migrant mid-April through May, then September to October. Also, see Red-tailed Hawk (page 162).

Adult.
Orange tail, belly band (usually darker than shown), brown head contrasting with white chest. Dark bar at leading edge of each underwing.

Juvenile.
Large and stocky, with broad dark belly band, white breast, and brown head. In flight, similar to adult but for pale tail with narrow dark bands.

RED-TAILED HAWK

Buteo jamaicensis Length: 22" / Wingspan: 50"

The Bay's most frequently seen and largest hawk, the "red-tail" begins pairing up for breeding just after the calendar page turns to a new year. Eggs are usually laid by March. As with the Red-shouldered Hawk, pairs frequently circle over their territory together, calling.

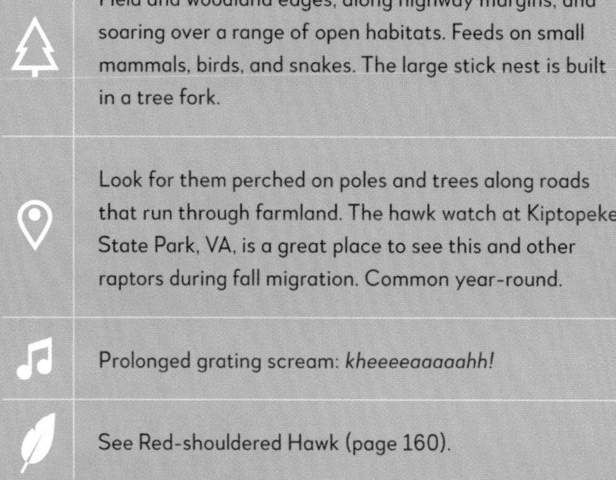

Field and woodland edges, along highway margins, and soaring over a range of open habitats. Feeds on small mammals, birds, and snakes. The large stick nest is built in a tree fork.

Look for them perched on poles and trees along roads that run through farmland. The hawk watch at Kiptopeke State Park, VA, is a great place to see this and other raptors during fall migration. Common year-round.

Prolonged grating scream: *kheeeeaaaaahh!*

See Red-shouldered Hawk (page 160).

Adult.
Black mask, cap, and hindneck. White throat and chest. Blackish back and fine black barring below.

Adult Merlin.
Heavy dark streaks below. Pale eyebrow. Less distinct facial pattern. Dark tail evenly banded with light gray.

PEREGRINE FALCON

Falco peregrinus Length: 16" / Wingspan: 41"

The Peregrine is widely considered the world's fastest diving bird, capable of reaching speeds of 200 miles per hour or faster during a stoop, or vertical dive. This swift predator also breaks into sudden horizontal pursuit, plowing into flocks of shorebirds, swallows, and doves.

Open habitats, often near wetlands where birds concentrate. Primarily eats birds, up to the size of small geese, but also catches bats and sometimes other small animals. In the Bay region, it nests on bridges, towers, and other structures.

Look for them at Kiptopeke State Park's hawk watch and at Eastern Shore of Virginia National Wildlife Refuge, VA. Uncommon, though more frequently seen around the few places where they nest and during fall migration, September–November.

Steady series of calls on the same pitch.

Smaller Merlin is an uncommon migrant and winter visitor.

Adult male.
Orange on back and tail. Bluish, black-spotted wings. Spotted chest and belly. Double-bar face pattern.

Adult female.
Barred rusty back and tail. Rusty streaks below. Double-bar face pattern.

AMERICAN KESTREL

Falco sparverius Length: 10.5" / Wingspan: 23"

This dove-sized open-country falcon was once called the "sparrow hawk." It has declined across the region, along with the Northern Bobwhite and Eastern Meadowlark.

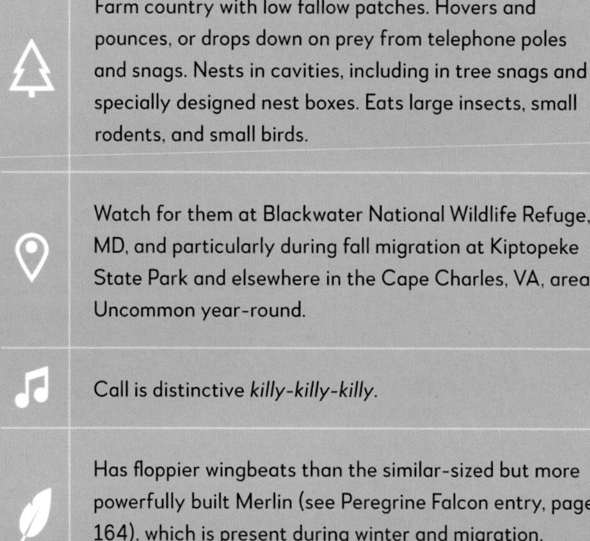

Farm country with low fallow patches. Hovers and pounces, or drops down on prey from telephone poles and snags. Nests in cavities, including in tree snags and specially designed nest boxes. Eats large insects, small rodents, and small birds.

Watch for them at Blackwater National Wildlife Refuge, MD, and particularly during fall migration at Kiptopeke State Park and elsewhere in the Cape Charles, VA, area. Uncommon year-round.

Call is distinctive *killy-killy-killy*.

Has floppier wingbeats than the similar-sized but more powerfully built Merlin (see Peregrine Falcon entry, page 164), which is present during winter and migration.

Adult.
Hornlike ear tufts and orange cheeks. Barred below.

Adult Barred Owl.
No ear tufts. Dark eyes. Barred breast over striped belly.

Adult Eastern Screech-Owl.
Small. Ear tufts and two white bars on wings. Gray color phase shown; red phase has fox-red coloration.

GREAT HORNED OWL

Bubo virginianus Length: 22" / Wingspan: 44"

One of the Bay's top avian predators is also one of its least-seen birds. But out of sight is never out of mind: its soft but penetrating hoots punctuate the night, even in winter, when these early nesters start laying eggs.

Found in deciduous and mixed forest. Uses former nests of hawks, eagles, herons, or crows, often in prominent tree forks. Eggs laid as early as January; young leave nest before May. Eats rodents, rabbits, skunks, birds, and other prey.

Watch for them at Marshy Point Nature Center and Blackwater National Wildlife Refuge, MD, and at Machicomoco State Park, VA.

Muffled *who whoo-oo who who*. Pairs often duet; female calls on higher pitch.

Barred Owl found in swamps and humid woods with large trees and has strident call: *who-cooks-for-you ... who-cooks-for-you-all*. Eastern Screech-Owl makes trills and whinnies.

Adults.
Tan with black wing spots and long, tapered tail.

Adult Rock Pigeons.
Plumage highly variable but most are gray or darker than Mourning Dove. Tail squared, not tapered. Typical plumage gray with two black wingbars, black tail band, and striking white rump visible in flight.

Adult Eurasian Collared-Dove.
Large and very pale, with black neck crescent. Bottom half of undertail is white. Tail tip squared, not tapered.

MOURNING DOVE

Zenaida macroura

Length: 12" / Wingspan: 18"

This elegant, taper-tailed dove delivers a soulful morning chorus from late winter into summer. During looping courtship glides, males resemble small soaring raptors. Look closely at this bird's neck to see flashes of iridescent green and a blush of pink.

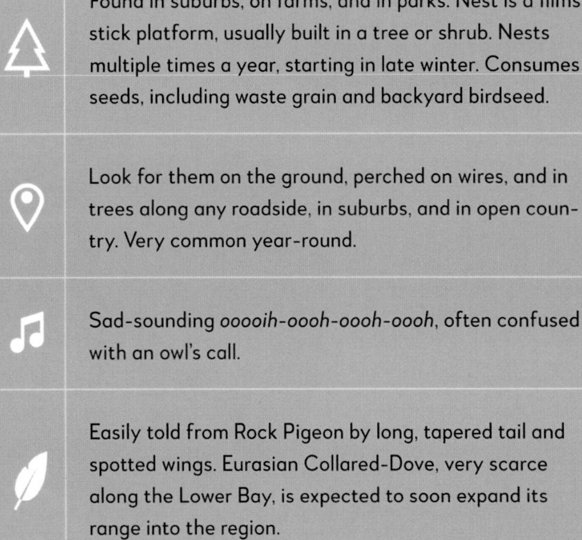

Found in suburbs, on farms, and in parks. Nest is a flimsy stick platform, usually built in a tree or shrub. Nests multiple times a year, starting in late winter. Consumes seeds, including waste grain and backyard birdseed.

Look for them on the ground, perched on wires, and in trees along any roadside, in suburbs, and in open country. Very common year-round.

Sad-sounding *ooooih-oooh-oooh-oooh*, often confused with an owl's call.

Easily told from Rock Pigeon by long, tapered tail and spotted wings. Eurasian Collared-Dove, very scarce along the Lower Bay, is expected to soon expand its range into the region.

Adult.
Curved yellow bill, rusty wingtips, and bold black-and-white undertail pattern.

Adult Black-billed Cuckoo.
Slightly curved blackish bill, red eyering; less white, less bold undertail pattern.

YELLOW-BILLED CUCKOO

Coccyzus americanus Length: 12" / Wingspan: 18"

Despite its curved banana-yellow bill and bold undertail pattern, this retiring bird is often hard to spot as it quietly perches or slips through dense foliage in an almost serpentine manner.

Deciduous and mixed forest and thickly vegetated edges. Diet includes many caterpillars, large insects like cicadas, and occasional small vertebrates. Nest is a flimsy twig platform placed in vine tangles or other dense cover.

Look for them at Eastern Shore of Virginia National Wildlife Refuge and First Landing State Park, VA, and at Eastern Neck and Blackwater National Wildlife Refuges, Elk Neck State Park, and Marshy Point Nature Center, MD. Fairly common May–October.

Distinctive *kuh-kih kuh-kih, kowl kowl kowl* song reveals this reclusive bird's presence. Also, repeated two-note, almost dove-like *ka-u, ka-u, ka-u.*

Black-billed Cuckoo an uncommon migrant and very scarce breeder in the region.

Adult male.
Ruby-red throat contrasts with white chest. Metallic green back, sides, and crown.

Adult female on nest.
Green back and head. Whitish throat.

Subadult male Rufous Hummingbird.
Dull orange belly wash and orangish on tail feathers.

RUBY-THROATED HUMMINGBIRD

Archilochus colubris

Length: 3.5" / Wingspan: 4.5"

Weighing just one-tenth of an ounce, this sprite is the Bay's smallest bird and its only nesting hummingbird. Its wings beat more than 50 times per second as it hovers. When it zips overhead, it can be mistaken for a large dragonfly or cicada.

Gardens, parks, and forest and wetland edges. Feeds on nectar, spiders, and insects including gnats and mosquitoes. Nest, hidden in a tree or shrub, is a small, tight cup of plant bits bound by spiderwebs and camouflaged with lichen and leaf fragments.

Look for them at Kiptopeke State Park, VA, and at Chesapeake Bay Environmental Center and North Point State Park, MD—and anywhere trumpet vine, jewelweed, and other nectar-rich blooms abound. Common mid-April–September.

Soft chatter: *twid-did-dit* or *twid-twid-twid*.

The more orangey Rufous Hummingbird is a rare visitor, usually in late fall and winter.

Male.
Ragged crest and dagger bill. Bluish above, with single bluish breastband.

Female.
Like male but with additional belt of rust-orange below the bluish breastband.

BELTED KINGFISHER

Megaceryle alcyon Length: 13" / Wingspan: 20"

Often seen on prominent perches overlooking wetlands, this pigeon-sized bird stands out thanks to its long, pointy bill, shaggy crest, and blue-gray breastband. Females have an additional orange belt.

Along creeks, rivers, marshes, lakes, ponds, swamps, and the Bay's shoreline. Hovers or drops down from a perch on small fish, but also frogs, crayfish, and insects. Nests in three- to six-foot-deep tunnels dug into eroded banks.

Look for them at Sandy Point State Park, Chesapeake Bay Environmental Center, North Beach marsh, and Blackwater National Wildlife Refuge, MD, and at Grandview Nature Preserve and Kiptopeke State Park, VA. Fairly common year-round.

Loud, insistent rattle that varies in length.

Easily identified by shape, behavior, and sound.

Male.
Crown and back of head scarlet. Zebra-striped back.

Female.
Like male but has grayish crown.

Adult Red-headed Woodpecker.
Entirely red head, glossy black back, and large white wing patches.

RED-BELLIED WOODPECKER

Melanerpes carolinus

Length: 9.25" / Wingspan: 16"

This bird's common name is misleading, given that the flashiest field marks are its scarlet head patch and zebra-striped back. The male's nape and crown are entirely red, while the female has a red hindneck and pale gray crown. Look carefully, though, and you may spot the namesake rosy blush on this bird's belly.

Tall deciduous and mixed forest, swamps, and suburbs. The varied diet includes grubs and other insects, small vertebrates, berries, suet, and seeds. Nests in a cavity excavated in a dead or dying tree.

Look for them in any forest, swamp, or wooded suburb. Also comes to backyard feeders. Common year-round.

Strident *clear clear clear*; also short, rapid rattle.

Red-headed Woodpecker is uncommon to scarce in the region.

Adult male.
Small with stubby bill and oblong white back patch. Male shows red on back of neck.

Adult male Hairy Woodpecker.
Markings similar to Downy but larger and with longer bill about the length of the head. Male shows red on back of neck.

Adult male Yellow-bellied Sapsucker.
White wing slash and barred back. Male has red throat (female's is white).

DOWNY WOODPECKER

Dryobates pubescens Length: 6.75" / Wingspan: 12"

North America's smallest woodpecker is most often seen on tree trunks and branches, but you may also spot this lightweight clinging to weedy stalks. It often feeds alongside other birds, including chickadees, titmice, nuthatches, and other woodpeckers.

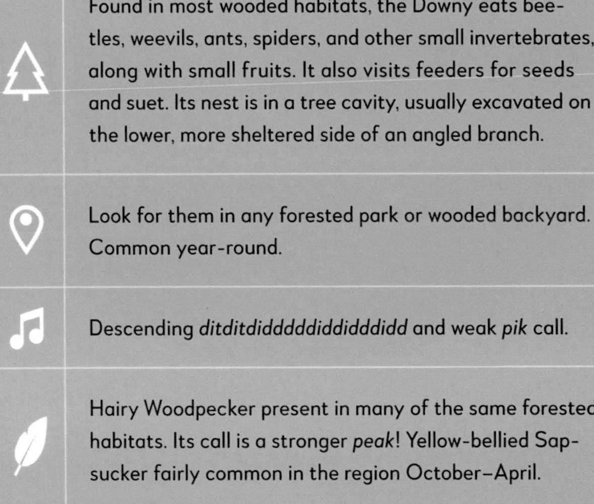

Found in most wooded habitats, the Downy eats beetles, weevils, ants, spiders, and other small invertebrates, along with small fruits. It also visits feeders for seeds and suet. Its nest is in a tree cavity, usually excavated on the lower, more sheltered side of an angled branch.

Look for them in any forested park or wooded backyard. Common year-round.

Descending *ditditdiddddiddidddidd* and weak *pik* call.

Hairy Woodpecker present in many of the same forested habitats. Its call is a stronger *peak*! Yellow-bellied Sapsucker fairly common in the region October–April.

Adult male.
Black breast crescent, gray nape with red wedge, and black spotting below. In flight, yellow wing linings and white rump are prominent. Female lacks black mustache.

NORTHERN FLICKER

Colaptes auratus Length: 12.5" / Wingspan: 20"

As it hops on the ground or takes to the air, this bird is a feast for the eyes, sporting spots and stripes, yellow underwings, and, in flight, a prominent white rump.

Open forest, parkland, swamps, and suburbs. Often seen on the ground feeding on ants and other insects; also consumes berries in trees and shrubs. Migrating birds pass overhead in numbers March and April, then September and October.

Look for them at Sandy Point and Point Lookout State Parks, MD, and especially during fall migration at Kiptopeke State Park and Eastern Shore of Virginia National Wildlife Refuge, VA, where hundreds may pass over in a day. Common year-round.

Song a long, steady series of notes on same pitch.
Call a piercing *tier*! Also, *wicka wicka wicka* call.

See Red-bellied Woodpecker (page 178).

Adult male.
Red-crested and crow-sized. Sexes colored alike, except male has red forehead (female's is blackish) and red mustache (female's is black).

PILEATED WOODPECKER

Dryocopus pileatus Length: 16.5" / Wingspan: 29"

This primeval-looking bird is the region's largest woodpecker. Piercing cries and heavy blows against hollow or rotting tree trunks will lead you to this fiery-crested beauty.

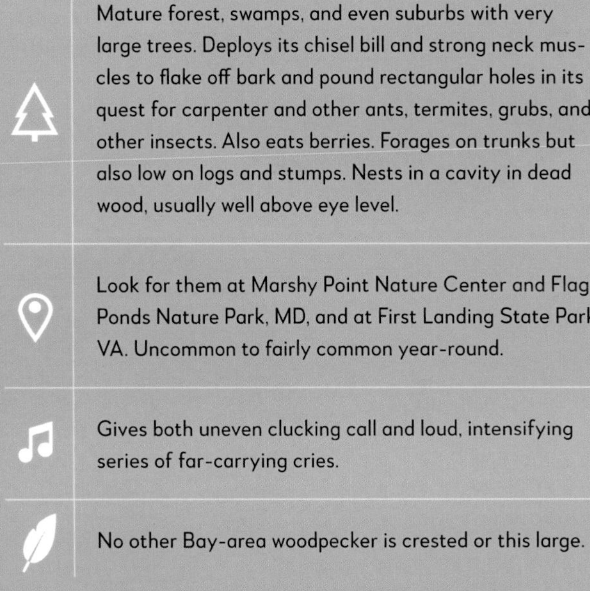

Mature forest, swamps, and even suburbs with very large trees. Deploys its chisel bill and strong neck muscles to flake off bark and pound rectangular holes in its quest for carpenter and other ants, termites, grubs, and other insects. Also eats berries. Forages on trunks but also low on logs and stumps. Nests in a cavity in dead wood, usually well above eye level.

Look for them at Marshy Point Nature Center and Flag Ponds Nature Park, MD, and at First Landing State Park, VA. Uncommon to fairly common year-round.

Gives both uneven clucking call and loud, intensifying series of far-carrying cries.

No other Bay-area woodpecker is crested or this large.

Adult.
Large flycatcher with bulky head, gray breast, and lemon-yellow underparts. Rusty orange on wings and tail.

Adult Ash-throated Flycatcher.
Much paler overall, especially the yellow.

GREAT CRESTED FLYCATCHER

Myiarchus crinitus Length: 8.75" / Wingspan: 13"

The Bay's largest and most colorful flycatcher proclaims its presence with a loud *weep*! Pairs often arrange shed snake skins around their nests, perhaps as a ruse to scare off predators.

Mixed and deciduous forest and edges. Sallies from a perch, hovers, or pounces on large insects including butterflies, moths, grasshoppers, crickets, beetles, and wasps. Nests in tree cavities, including old woodpecker holes, and sometimes in nest boxes, mailboxes, and rotting fence posts.

Look for them at Marshy Point Nature Center and Calvert Cliffs State Park, MD, and at Sandy Bottom Nature Park and First Landing State Park, VA. Common from late April–September.

Call is plaintive, loud *weep!* or *weep-weep-weep-weep*.

Ash-throated Flycatcher recalls a faded version of this species. It is a rare visitor, usually in late fall or winter, when Great Crested is absent.

Adult.
Blackish above and white below, with white tail tip.

EASTERN KINGBIRD

Tyrannus tyrannus Length: 8.5" / Wingspan: 15"

This two-toned songbird leads a double life: it zealously protects territory and mainly feasts on invertebrates while nesting, yet on South American wintering grounds it mostly eats small fruits and gathers in flocks, often with Tropical Kingbirds and Fork-tailed Flycatchers.

Open parkland, meadows with scattered trees, and forest and wetland edges. Sallies from a perch to capture insects large and small; also hovers then grabs prey. Eats some berries during spring and summer. The nest, made of twigs, forbs, and roots, sits high in a tree, sometimes fully exposed to elements.

Look for them at Eastern Neck National Wildlife Refuge and Terrapin Nature Park, MD, and at Fort Monroe, VA. Common from mid-April into September.

Sounds irritated. Detected in treetops by rapid calls, starting with staccato *tzeek* calls.

Not easily confused with any other Bay species.

Adult.
Greenish above and whitish below, with long extension on wing-tips. Thin eyering. All *Empidonax* flycatchers have two wingbars.

Adult Willow Flycatcher.
White throat stands out from smudgy breast. Lacks pale eyering. Medium extension of wingtips (primaries). Unless heard, not easily separated from Alder Flycatcher.

Adult Least Flycatcher.
Grayer above, with wide eyering, shorter bill, and shorter wingtips (primaries).

ACADIAN FLYCATCHER

Empidonax virescens Length: 5.75" / Wingspan: 9"

Belonging to the challenging *Empidonax* genus, this olive-green flycatcher is easiest to identify by its distinctive, short song.

Mature deciduous and mixed forest, often by swamps and streams. Perches low in the shadows, sallying for insects and spiders. The nest is a shaggy cup of twigs, forbs, and other vegetation, cemented with spider and caterpillar webs and affixed to a thin branch fork of a low tree.

Look for them at Franklin Point, North Point, and Calvert Cliffs State Parks, MD, and Machicomoco State Park, VA. Common on the Western Shore May–September; fairly common in suitable habitat on Eastern Shore.

Song is loud, brief *pit-SEUP!*

Willow Flycatcher is a scarce breeder. During migration, Least Flycatchers pass through, as do, with less frequency, Alder and Yellow-bellied Flycatchers (not shown). See also Eastern Wood-Pewee (in Eastern Phoebe entry on page 192).

Adult.
Blackish head with gray back and sides of breast. No wingbars.

Adult Eastern Wood-Pewee.
Whitish wingbars, grayish vest.

EASTERN PHOEBE

Sayornis phoebe Length: 7" / Wingspan: 10.5"

This is the Bay's only regularly wintering flycatcher (although in small numbers), and it's the first to appear in spring and last to leave in fall.

Vegetation fringing freshwater wetlands, along wooded streams, and at forest edges. Feeds low, flying from a perch to nab invertebrates in the air, on leaves, or on the ground. When perched, pumps its tail up and down. The fairly large mud and moss nest is often placed on a bridge, low building ledge, or dock.

Look for them at Marshy Point Nature Center, MD. Very common fall migrant in Cape Charles, VA. Common March–November; uncommon to scarce in winter.

Song is lazy *freedih ... freebee*. Year-round, utters a rather thin chip call.

Eastern Wood-Pewee has clear wingbars, doesn't pump tail, and frequently sings its name: *peeweeeee*. See also Acadian Flycatcher (page 190).

Adult.
Yellow "spectacle" surrounds white eye. Yellow sides and flanks. Pale throat and white wingbars. Juveniles have dark eyes.

Adult Eastern Warbling-Vireo.
A grayish bird with subtle face pattern lacking yellow. Has a dark eye and no wingbars.

Adult Blue-headed Vireo.
White goggles and throat contrast with otherwise dark gray head. Two white wingbars.

WHITE-EYED VIREO

Vireo griseus

Length: 5" / Wingspan: 7.5"

Though colorful and active, this bird is more often heard than seen, belting out its lively song from within dense tangles.

Thickets, scrub, and viny tangles. Eats a wide variety of insects and spiders, and some berries. Nest is a pouch made of leaves, bark, rootlets, and other materials suspended from a thin tree or shrub fork, often close to the ground.

Look for them at Point Lookout and Calvert Cliffs State Parks, MD, and at Kiptopeke State Park, VA. Fairly common from mid-April through September.

Song is peppy *per-chick-a-wow-chick!* Also, scold-like call: *rreeear*.

Eastern Warbling-Vireo a common breeder in Upper Bay. Philadelphia Vireo (not shown) a rather scarce fall migrant; it is similar to Eastern Warbling-Vireo but has yellow throat and darker eyestripe. Blue-headed Vireo a fairly common migrant early in spring and fairly late in fall.

Adult.
Flatter-headed and longer-billed than region's other vireos, with blackish stripe through eye and below gray crown. No wingbars. Red eye (brown in immature, not shown).

Adult Yellow-throated Vireo.
Yellow head, breast, and goggles. Two white wingbars.

RED-EYED VIREO

Vireo olivaceus Length: 6" / Wingspan: 10"

After wintering in the Amazon basin, this vireo returns to anchor the forest's birdsong chorus. Often hidden in leafy treetops, it is seldom seen for such a common bird.

Deciduous and mixed forest. Gleans a wide variety of insects and spiders; also eats small fruits such as dogwood berries. Nest, made of grasses, twigs, forbs, and even parts of paper-wasp nests, is an open cup fastened to a thin branch fork.

Look for them at Marshy Point Nature Center and Franklin Point and North Point State Parks, MD, and at Hughlett Point Natural Area Preserve, VA. Common late April–October.

Song recalls robin's song, but with less gusto: "hurry up, here I go" repeated seemingly endlessly, even through hot summer afternoons. Call sounds annoyed: *vvreaah*.

Yellow-throated Vireo song similar but raspier, with longer pauses between phrases that often sound like "three-eight."

Adult.
Powder-blue back and crest. Black collar. Wings checkered in mosaic-like pattern of blue, white, and black. White tail corners flash in flight.

BLUE JAY

Cyanocitta cristata Length: 11" / Wingspan: 16"

This crow family member plays roles of town crier, predator, farmer, and beauty pageant winner. Jays sound the alarm on other predators but raid nests themselves. They cache tree nuts, unwittingly planting some. Though easy to take for granted, they are gorgeous.

Deciduous and mixed forest. Feeds on insects, seeds and tree nuts, berries, nestlings and other small animals, eggs, and sometimes carrion. The twiggy nest is placed in a tree at variable height.

Look for them in backyards, parks, forests, and edges. Very common year-round. Regional migrations make it difficult to know if the jays you see in winter are the same ones present in summer.

Jay! Jay! Jay! (as if calling its own name) but also variety of other sounds, including imitations of Red-shouldered and Red-tailed Hawk calls.

There are no other crested, blue birds in the region.

Adult.
Large, all black, with squared tail (especially apparent in flight).

American Crow in flight.

Adult Common Raven.
As large as Red-tailed Hawk—but size comparison difficult if not seen alongside crows. Very long wings, almost diamond-shaped tail, and very large bill. Unlike crows, often soars like a raptor.

AMERICAN CROW

Corvus brachyrhynchos Length: 17.5" / Wingspan: 39"

Roosting in large numbers fall through winter, crows pair off in spring to raise their young. These intelligent birds can recognize individual humans they fear or associate with food.

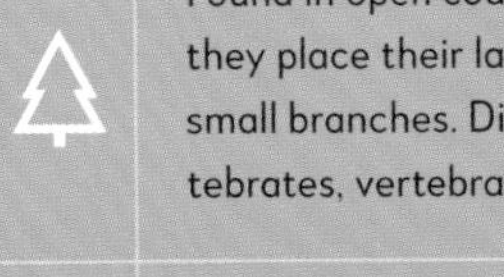

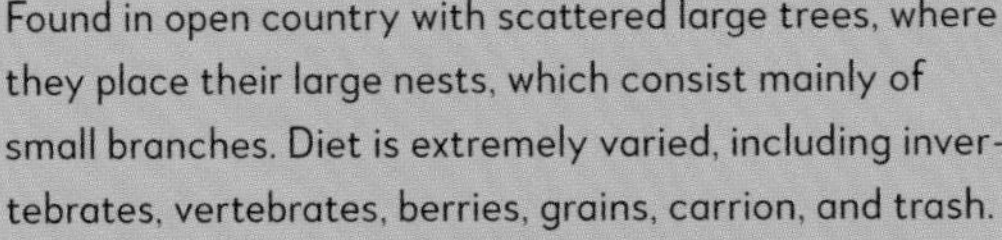

Found in open country with scattered large trees, where they place their large nests, which consist mainly of small branches. Diet is extremely varied, including invertebrates, vertebrates, berries, grains, carrion, and trash.

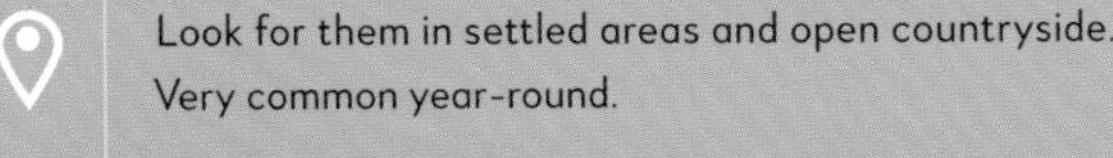

Look for them in settled areas and open countryside. Very common year-round.

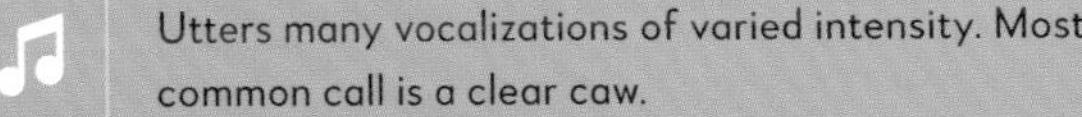

Utters many vocalizations of varied intensity. Most common call is a clear caw.

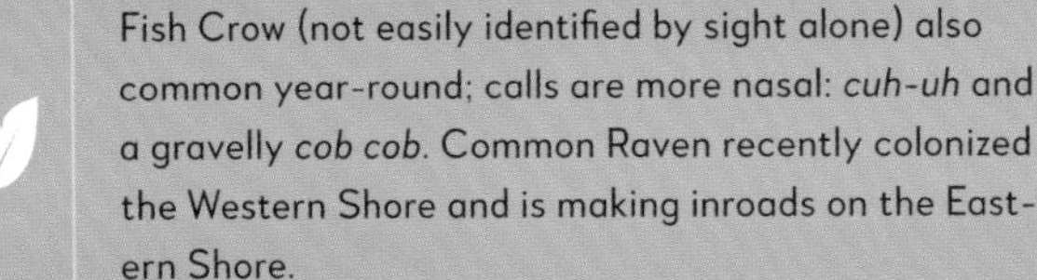

Fish Crow (not easily identified by sight alone) also common year-round; calls are more nasal: *cuh-uh* and a gravelly *cob cob*. Common Raven recently colonized the Western Shore and is making inroads on the Eastern Shore.

Adult.
Brownish olive back. Dingy buff below. No bold wing markings but may show pale edges. Subtle grayish tinge to back of cheek.

Adult Black-capped Chickadee.
Inverted white "hockey stick" pattern usually visible on wings. Buffy sides (not shown here) contrast white on breast and belly. White back of cheek.

CAROLINA CHICKADEE

Poecile carolinensis Length: 4.75" / Wingspan: 7.5"

Outside nesting season, this perky black-bibbed songbird and the Tufted Titmouse anchor mixed-species feeding flocks that often include nuthatches, kinglets, creepers, and warblers.

Deciduous and mixed woods, backyards, and parks. Nest, placed within a cavity in decaying wood or in a nest box, is a small but bulky mass of coarse moss and bark topped with soft fur and plant fibers. Eats caterpillars, spiders, other invertebrates, seeds, and berries.

Look for them at Sandy Point State Park and Blackwater National Wildlife Refuge, MD, and at Sandy Bottom Nature Park and First Landing State Park, VA. Common year-round. Comes to feeders for black oil sunflower seed and suet.

Call is rapid *chickadee-dee-dee*. Song is high-pitched, whistled *feebee, feebay*.

Black-capped Chickadee rarely strays to the region in late fall and winter. Call slower but similar to Carolina's; song is sweet, loud *fee-bee ... fee-bee*.

Adult.
Small gray bird with crest, black forehead and eye, and orange sides. Immature often lacks black on forehead, and sides are washed in paler orange.

TUFTED TITMOUSE

Baeolophus bicolor Length: 6.5" / Wingspan: 9.75"

Along with the Carolina Chickadee, Carolina Wren, and Northern Cardinal, the Tufted Titmouse is one of relatively few Bay songbirds to remain in the same place all year long. It has been suggested that in addition to anchoring mixed-species flocks, this nonmigratory bird's presence indicates quality habitat for other birds.

Deciduous and mixed woods, and suburbs and parks with an abundance of large trees. Nests in old woodpecker holes, natural cavities, and sometimes nest boxes. Eats insects, seeds, nuts, and berries. Often associates with Carolina Chickadees and other small birds. Visits feeders.

Look for them in well-wooded suburbs and parks, including at North Point State Park, MD, and at Kiptopeke State Park, VA. Common year-round.

Song is ringing *peter, peter, peter, peter*. Call is toned-down *chee-chee-taw*. Also: *chee-keer*.

The only crested gray bird in the region, but see Cedar Waxwing (page 218).

Adult.
Yellowish face with black mask and collar. Curly "hornlike" crest. Dirt-colored back. Hunched posture.

Nonbreeding American Pipit.
Grayish-brown above and streaked below, with straight, longish bill and long tail. White outer tail feathers flash in flight.

Nonbreeding Snow Bunting.
White below and on wings. No streaks below. Cinnamon patches on head and sides of breast. Triangular orangish bill.

Nonbreeding Lapland Longspur.
Dark-outlined ear patch; often noticeable rust color on wings and collar. Sparrow-like shape.

HORNED LARK

Eremophila alpestris Length: 7" / Wingspan: 12"

The country's only native lark is easily overlooked as it hunkers down in expansive open habitats.

Treeless stretches with bare ground or very low vegetation, including plowed and just-planted farm fields, pastures, sod farms, runways, and shorelines. Eats seeds and small invertebrates. During courtship flights, males hover, circle, and sing. The bowl-shaped nest lies in a dip in the soil and is made of grasses and forbs.

Look for them in farm country, such as near Blackwater National Wildlife Refuge, MD, and near Eastern Shore of Virginia National Wildlife Refuge, VA. Fairly common year-round.

The jumbled, tinkling song is a great way to locate these birds from late winter into summer.

American Pipit and, with less frequency, Snow Bunting and Lapland Longspur, sometimes forage in the same fields as Horned Larks.

Adult.
Cinder gray, often darker on belly and undertail. Sickle-winged, with tail that's neither forked nor notched.

CHIMNEY SWIFT

Chaetura pelagica Length: 5.25" / Wingspan: 14"

Frenetic and almost bat-like in flight, this ash-colored aerial insectivore skitters overhead but breaks into an I-formation glide during courtship flights.

Hunts entirely on the wing, snapping up winged insects including flies, beetles, moths, and flying ants. Nests mostly in chimneys and uninhabited buildings, where shaded vertical walls provide surfaces for their semi-circular twig nests, which are bound and cemented using the birds' sticky saliva.

Widespread but declining. Watch for them over towns and cities, but also fields and water's edge. Common mid-April into October.

Persistent, distinctive chittering.

Superfi cially similar but unrelated swallows routinely perch on wires, trees, and reeds, which swifts are unable to do, and have quick but more fluid wingbeats.

Adult male.
Metallic bluish-green above and all-white below. Female's back color varies from dull to almost as colorful as male's.

Juvenile or dull-colored adult female.
Dark brown-gray on back and head; often has smudgy gray on breast.

Adult Northern Rough-winged Swallow.
Mostly brown with brownish throat, chest, and sides and whitish belly and vent (undertail).

Adult Bank Swallow.
Wet sand color on back and head. White below with dark chest band. Pointy tail with slight fork. The region's smallest swallow, with the most frenetic flight.

TREE SWALLOW

Tachycineta bicolor Length: 5.75" / Wingspan: 14.5"

Swallows are known for hawking flying insects, but this species also eats berries during cold months, enabling it to winter farther north than its relatives.

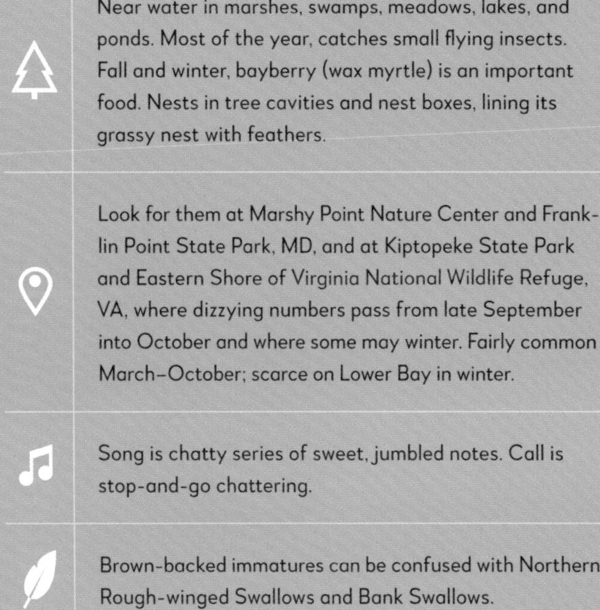

Near water in marshes, swamps, meadows, lakes, and ponds. Most of the year, catches small flying insects. Fall and winter, bayberry (wax myrtle) is an important food. Nests in tree cavities and nest boxes, lining its grassy nest with feathers.

Look for them at Marshy Point Nature Center and Franklin Point State Park, MD, and at Kiptopeke State Park and Eastern Shore of Virginia National Wildlife Refuge, VA, where dizzying numbers pass from late September into October and where some may winter. Fairly common March–October; scarce on Lower Bay in winter.

Song is chatty series of sweet, jumbled notes. Call is stop-and-go chattering.

Brown-backed immatures can be confused with Northern Rough-winged Swallows and Bank Swallows.

Adult male.
All dark. Inky, shiny blue-black. Tail notched when closed.

Female/immature.
Dark on head often extends to breast; noticeably lighter below—can be whitish or grayish.

PURPLE MARTIN

Progne subis Length: 8" / Wingspan: 18"

The country's largest swallow and, in the case of adult males, the only all-dark one. In flight, this species can be identified from quite a distance, thanks to its heavier wingbeats and frequent glides. Purple Martins often forage higher up than other swallows.

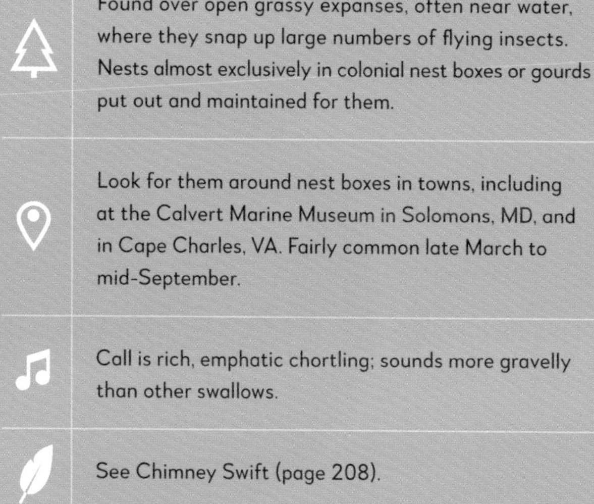

Found over open grassy expanses, often near water, where they snap up large numbers of flying insects. Nests almost exclusively in colonial nest boxes or gourds put out and maintained for them.

Look for them around nest boxes in towns, including at the Calvert Marine Museum in Solomons, MD, and in Cape Charles, VA. Fairly common late March to mid-September.

Call is rich, emphatic chortling; sounds more gravelly than other swallows.

See Chimney Swift (page 208).

Adult.
Orange or pale orange below with long, deeply forked tail. Brick-red throat. Metallic-blue back. Immature has much shorter tail.

Adult Cliff Swallow.
Squared tail, pale rump and collar, and white forehead.

BARN SWALLOW

Hirundo rustica Length: 6.75" / Wingspan: 15"

With its long scissor tail and airborne agility, this metallic-blue and orange bird is one of the world's best known and most beloved swallows. This and other aerial insectivores have declined, as pesticides cut back their prey and small farms with livestock give way to industrial farms and subdivisions.

Cruises low and snaps up flying insects over pastures, fallow fields, and playing fields. Pairs build a rounded mud-and-grass nest on a ledge or under a bridge or culvert. Does not nest in colonies.

Look for them over many open areas, including at Marshy Point Nature Center, Franklin Point State Park, and Terrapin Nature Park, MD, and at Windmill Point, VA. Fairly common April–September.

Song is continuous, chatty ramble. Call, given in flight, is *vip*.

Cliff Swallow an uncommon migrant and localized breeder in the Bay region.

Adult male flashing crown patch.
Bold white eyering. Wide wingbar. Male has ruby-red crown patch (seldom seen). Short tail.

Adult male Golden-crowned Kinglet.
Orange-and-yellow crown (just yellow in female), fringed with black. Crown patch always visible. Dark line through eye. Wide wingbar. Short tail.

RUBY-CROWNED KINGLET

Corthylio calendula

Length: 4.25" / Wingspan: 7.5"

Despite being just over four inches long, this tiny, short-tailed bundle of energy captures attention thanks to its distinctive call and song, its "nervous" wing flicks, and its bold white eye-ring and wingbar. Often seen foraging alongside chickadees, titmice, nuthatches, and warblers. When agitated, the male sometimes flashes his scarlet crown patch.

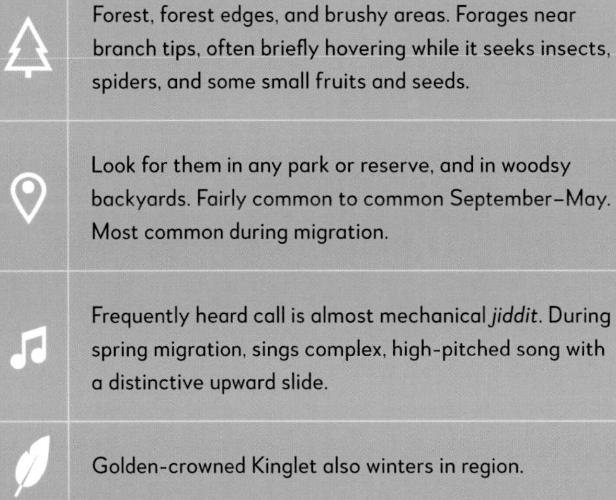

Forest, forest edges, and brushy areas. Forages near branch tips, often briefly hovering while it seeks insects, spiders, and some small fruits and seeds.

Look for them in any park or reserve, and in woodsy backyards. Fairly common to common September–May. Most common during migration.

Frequently heard call is almost mechanical *jiddit*. During spring migration, sings complex, high-pitched song with a distinctive upward slide.

Golden-crowned Kinglet also winters in region.

Adult.
Crested and caramel colored, with black mask and yellow-tipped gray tail. Yellowish belly. In adults, namesake waxy red wing spots are often visible, if you look carefully.

CEDAR WAXWING

Bombycilla cedrorum Length: 7.25" / Wingspan: 12"

Masked, crested, and colorful, this songbird is usually seen in flocks, either overhead or in berry-bearing trees, shrubs, or vines.

Suburbs and parks, forest edges, and open areas with scattered trees.

Look for them at Sandy Point State Park, Pickering Creek Audubon Center, and Eastern Neck National Wildlife Refuge, MD, and at Eastern Shore of Virginia National Wildlife Refuge, VA. Fairly common year-round, but presence varies season to season, year to year.

High-pitched raspy *zeee*, often given simultaneously as a flock flies overhead.

This bird is distinctive, although Tufted Titmouse, Blue Jay, and Northern Cardinal are also crested.

Adult male.
Black cap does not extend to eyes. Bluish back. White below with rusty vent. Female has dark gray cap.

Adult male Red-breasted Nuthatch.
Striped head, orange below, with bluish back. Female has dark gray cap.

WHITE-BREASTED NUTHATCH

Sitta carolinensis Length: 5.75" / Wingspan: 11"

Creeping up and down large deciduous tree trunks and branches, this bluish-backed, white-bellied bird often gives away its presence with nasal *yank, yank, yank* calls. Likely named after its feeding behavior—hacking seeds and nuts it wedges into crevices—this bird often joins mixed-species foraging flocks "led" by chickadees and titmice.

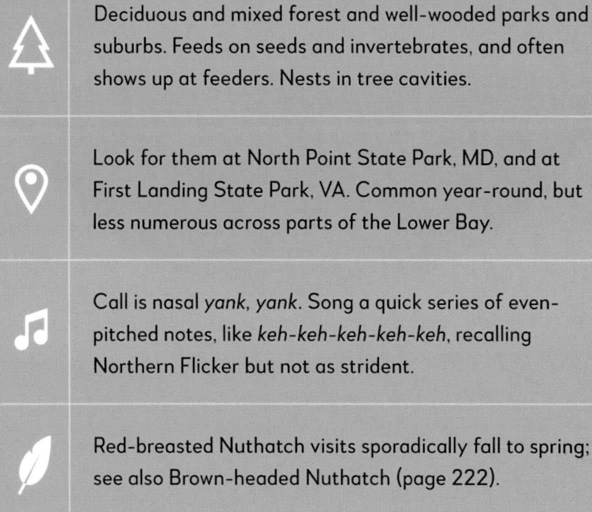

Deciduous and mixed forest and well-wooded parks and suburbs. Feeds on seeds and invertebrates, and often shows up at feeders. Nests in tree cavities.

Look for them at North Point State Park, MD, and at First Landing State Park, VA. Common year-round, but less numerous across parts of the Lower Bay.

Call is nasal *yank, yank*. Song a quick series of even-pitched notes, like *keh-keh-keh-keh-keh*, recalling Northern Flicker but not as strident.

Red-breasted Nuthatch visits sporadically fall to spring; see also Brown-headed Nuthatch (page 222).

Adult.
Brown cap extending down to eyes.

BROWN-HEADED NUTHATCH

Sitta pusilla Length: 4.5" / Wingspan: 7.75"

Stubby-tailed and social, this pine-loving bird reaches its northern range limit in the Bay region. It is one of the few known tool-using birds—sometimes using bark chip wedges to pry off other bark and reveal prey—and is one of North America's few cooperatively breeding species, with non-parent birds assisting with nesting duties.

Loblolly pine forest, often near wetland edges. Often in small groups, clambering on pine cones and branches alongside chickadees and others. Eats insects, spiders, and seeds. Nests in cavities, mostly in dead pines.

Look for them at Eastern Neck and Blackwater National Wildlife Refuges, Chesapeake Bay Environmental Center, and Point Lookout State Park, MD, and at many Lower Bay sites in VA. Common year-round in the mid to Lower Bay.

Listen for this bird's distinctive squeaky-toy calls.

See White-breasted and Red-breasted Nuthatches (page 220).

Adult.
Thin, sickle-like bill and long tail, with bark-patterned back. Whitish below.

BROWN CREEPER

Certhia americana Length: 5.25" / Wingspan: 7.75"

Its back the color of bark, this is a well-camouflaged and easy-to-miss species. The best way to find this bird among mixed foraging flocks is to listen for its high-pitched call.

Deciduous, pine, and mixed forests. The bird starts at the base of a trunk, slowly spirals upward toward the crown, then drops low to another trunk. Inspects crevices and flaked bark for insects and spiders. Sometimes visits suet feeders.

Look for them at Blackwater National Wildlife Refuge and North Point State Park, MD, and at Newport News Park and First Landing State Park, VA. Fairly common October–April; rarely stays to nest.

Call a high-pitched *tzeeet*.

This small, curved-billed bird is not usually confused for any other tree-climbing species.

Breeding male.
Dull blue above, with long, cocked black-and-white tail. White eyering. Breeding males have black eyebrow line.

BLUE-GRAY GNATCATCHER

Polioptila caerulea Length: 4.5" / Wingspan: 6"

This dusty-blue sprite is one of the Bay's smallest breeding birds, after the hummingbird. It returns to forests early in spring, before leaves fully emerge, and pairs soon set to work crafting their tiny nests.

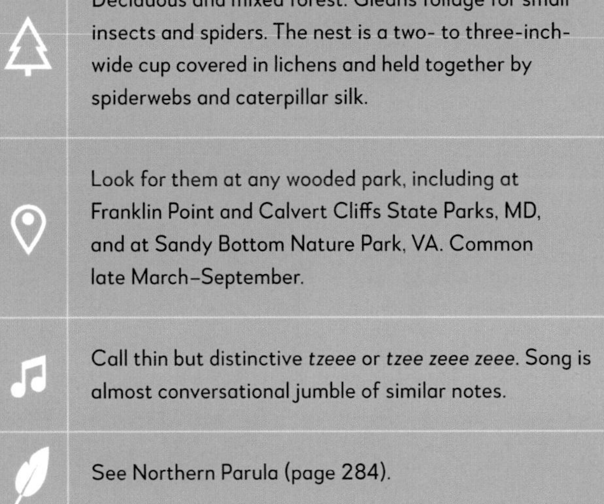

Deciduous and mixed forest. Gleans foliage for small insects and spiders. The nest is a two- to three-inch-wide cup covered in lichens and held together by spiderwebs and caterpillar silk.

Look for them at any wooded park, including at Franklin Point and Calvert Cliffs State Parks, MD, and at Sandy Bottom Nature Park, VA. Common late March–September.

Call thin but distinctive *tzeee* or *tzee zeee zeee*. Song is almost conversational jumble of similar notes.

See Northern Parula (page 284).

Adult.
Bold white eyebrow. Orangey below, with rufous back and tail. Curved bill and cocked tail.

Adult Marsh Wren.
White eyebrow. Narrow white barring across back. Whitish throat and chest contrast with brown flanks. Curved bill and cocked tail.

CAROLINA WREN

Thryothorus ludovicianus Length: 5.5" / Wingspan: 7.5"

Carolina Wrens are the neighborhood watch of the undergrowth, issuing alarm calls at any sign of trouble. In spring and early summer, family bands roam the foliage. By fall, singles and couples remain, often foraging near other birds.

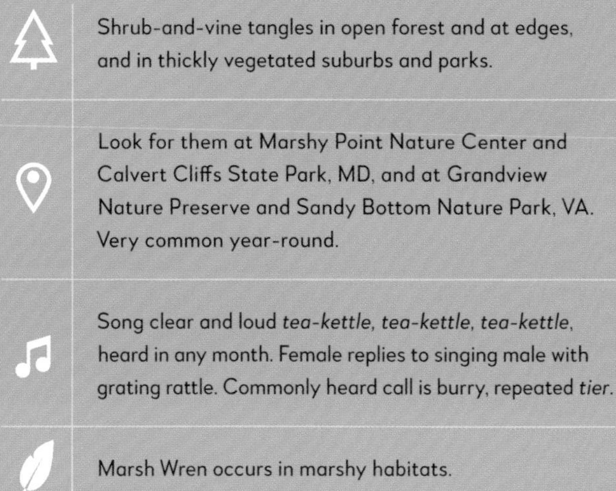

Shrub-and-vine tangles in open forest and at edges, and in thickly vegetated suburbs and parks.

Look for them at Marshy Point Nature Center and Calvert Cliffs State Park, MD, and at Grandview Nature Preserve and Sandy Bottom Nature Park, VA. Very common year-round.

Song clear and loud *tea-kettle, tea-kettle, tea-kettle*, heard in any month. Female replies to singing male with grating rattle. Commonly heard call is burry, repeated *tier*.

Marsh Wren occurs in marshy habitats.

Adult.
Finely barred wings and tail, indistinct face pattern. Below, pale brown and unmarked except for barring on vent.

Adult Winter Wren.
Round body, with blackish barring on flanks and stubby, upturned tail.

NORTHERN HOUSE WREN

Troglodytes aedon Length: 4.75" / Wingspan: 6"

Tiny but mighty, this jabbering little songbird relentlessly investigates nesting places, sometimes evicting bluebirds and others, dumping out their eggs and young. It will also kill wasps and remove their nests to make way for its own.

Low in thick brush edging forests and yards. Creeps through foliage and along shaded ground to capture insects, spiders, and millipedes. The nest, built within a cavity, is a mass of sticks, within which sits a cup of grasses, forbs, and other soft materials. The male often starts several nests and the female selects one.

Listen and look for them in leafy backyards, gardens, and parks. Common mid-April through October; scarce to uncommon on Lower Bay in winter.

Song a complex jumble of notes, usually starting level, then speeding up and dropping at the end.

Winter Wren is an uncommon visitor October–April.

Adult.
Gray (almost bluish gray) with a black cap and rusty undertail.

GRAY CATBIRD

Dumetella carolinensis

Length: 8.5" / Wingspan: 11"

The catbird's vocal organ, or syrinx, is highly developed, allowing it to sing "with two voices." Its scratchy, varied song, sounding as if the bird is constantly talking to itself, is frequently heard predawn and throughout the day.

Brushy deciduous and mixed forest, scrub, suburbs, and parks. Forages low on branches and on the ground for insects and spiders; also eats berries. Cup nest is made of twigs, grasses, forbs, and leaves, hidden in a shrub, low tree, or vine tangle, often at or just above eye level.

Look for them in shaded suburbs and parkland throughout the region. Common late April through October; scarce to uncommon (Lower Bay) in winter.

Song a rambling, variable string of sounds, punctuated with catlike mews. Calls: namesake *mew*; *rat-ta-tat* alarm call; shorter *kwaht*.

Coloration is distinctive.

Adult.
Rusty orange tail, back, and nape with heavy dark streaking below. Two thin whitish wingbars and lemon-yellow eyes.

BROWN THRASHER

Toxostoma rufum Length: 11.5" / Wingspan: 13"

Except when males sing in spring, this almost fox-orange mockingbird relative usually remains hunkered down in the shadows, thrashing its bill back and forth like a scythe as it works the leaf litter for hidden invertebrates.

Open woods, hedgerows, and forest edges with dense undergrowth. Feeds on insects, spiders, snails, berries, seeds, and tree nuts, including acorns. Bulky nest, made of leaves, twigs, bark, stalks, and grasses, is often fastened low in a dense shrub or young tree.

Look for them at Grandview Nature Preserve, VA, and at Eastern Neck National Wildlife Refuge and Chesapeake Environmental Center, MD. Fairly common April–November; scarce to uncommon (parts of Lower Bay) in winter.

Song a varied stream of paired or triple notes, recalling mockingbird, but less boisterous and with shorter repetitions.

See Wood Thrush (page 244).

Adult.
Pale gray head and back. Long tail. White wing patches and outer tail feathers flash in flight.

Juvenile.
Spotted breast fades as bird grows to adult size.

NORTHERN MOCKINGBIRD

Mimus polyglottos Length: 10" / Wingspan: 14"

Famed for imitating other birds' songs and other sounds, this boisterous, flashy member of the thrasher family also has the distinction of being one of the Bay's few songbirds to sometimes sing at night.

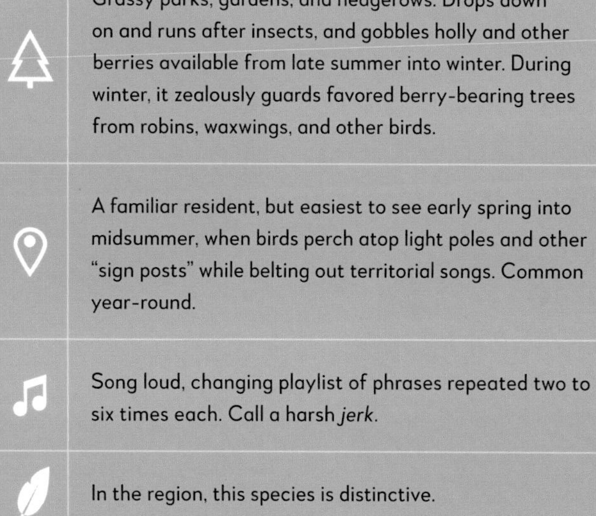

Grassy parks, gardens, and hedgerows. Drops down on and runs after insects, and gobbles holly and other berries available from late summer into winter. During winter, it zealously guards favored berry-bearing trees from robins, waxwings, and other birds.

A familiar resident, but easiest to see early spring into midsummer, when birds perch atop light poles and other "sign posts" while belting out territorial songs. Common year-round.

Song loud, changing playlist of phrases repeated two to six times each. Call a harsh *jerk*.

In the region, this species is distinctive.

Breeding adult.
Glossy green with purplish gleam on breast and neck. Yellow bill.

Nonbreeding adult.
Frosty head with dark pointy bill. Body covered in snowflake-like spots.

Molting juvenile.
Juveniles are tan with pale throats. This one is molting: body is in new, adult plumage but head remains in juvenile plumage.

EUROPEAN STARLING

Sturnus vulgaris Length: 8.5" / Wingspan: 16"

An eye-catching bird related to mynas, the starling glints iridescent purple and green in spring and is dotted with white from fall into winter.

Suburbs, cities, swamps with dead or dying trees, and farms. Starlings insert their long bills into soft turf then force them open in the soil, exposing grubs, worms, and other prey. They also eat seeds and berries. Nest is a bulky collection of twigs, stems, grasses, and other materials stuffed into a cavity, such as in a streetlight fixture or woodpecker hole.

Easy to find in cities and suburbs. In fall and winter, gathers in twisting, cloudlike flocks called murmurations. Very common year-round.

Song is a rambling, gurgling mix of notes with some bird-call imitations thrown in.

Unlike blackbirds, starlings wear white spots fall to winter and sport yellow bills in spring and summer.

Adult male.
Sky-blue back, wings, and head with orange on breast, sides, neck, and throat.

Adult female.
Blue wings and tail, with bluish or grayish on head. Orange breast, sides, and neck.

Juvenile.
Brown with white spots and some light blue on wings and tail.

EASTERN BLUEBIRD

Sialia sialis

Length: 7" / Wingspan: 13"

Despite competition from introduced House Sparrows and European Starlings, the bluebird remains a common sight thanks to decades of nest box installation and monitoring, and forestry practices that leave dead standing trees.

Fields, clearings, woodland edges, and parkland. Drops from a wire or branch to the ground to grab grasshoppers, crickets, caterpillars, and spiders; also eats berries. Nest is a bulky cup usually made of grasses or pine needles, built in a nest box or tree cavity. Usually seen in pairs or small flocks.

Look for them at Marshy Point Nature Center and Franklin Point State Park, MD, and at First Landing State Park, VA, and on power lines running through farm country. Common year-round.

Song a sweet ramble: *cheer-churry-churple*. Call a distinctive *churr*, singly or in a series.

No other Bay songbird has blue-and-orange coloration.

Adult.
Warm olive-brown above with contrasting reddish tail. Dark spotting on breast. Thin eyering.

Adult Swainson's Thrush.
Buffy wash to head, including distinct buffy goggles. Dark spotting on breast. Tail same brown color as back.

Adult Gray-cheeked Thrush.
Dark brown on back and head. No distinct eyering. Heavy black spotting on breast. (Bicknell's Thrush, not shown, is virtually identical to more-common Gray-cheeked.)

HERMIT THRUSH

Catharus guttatus Length: 6.75" / Wingspan: 11.5"

The only spot-breasted, brown-backed thrush to winter around the Bay. True to its name, this bird is retiring and easily overlooked. They defend winter territories from others of their species, but will mingle with robins and other foraging birds.

Thickets and tangles at forest edges and woods with thick leaf litter and scattered hollies. Forages on the ground for insects, spiders, and earthworms; takes to the trees, shrubs, and vines to pluck berries.

Look for them at Sandy Point and Calvert Cliffs State Parks, MD, and at First Landing and Kiptopeke State Parks, VA. Uncommon to fairly common October–early May.

Calls: nasal, rising *vreeet* and *bib* or *bib-bib*. Does not usually sing its flute-like song fall through winter.

In May and September–October, Swainson's, Gray-cheeked, and Bicknell's Thrushes and Veery move through, posing identification challenges.

Adult.
Rich orangey brown on head, back, wings, and tail. Large black spots pepper white underparts.

WOOD THRUSH

Hylocichla mustelina Length: 7.75" / Wingspan: 13"

In spring, this spot-breasted songster returns to Bay area forests after wintering in Central America and southern Mexico. Its ringing song accompanies the territorial proclamations of other arriving Neotropical migrants and Bay nesters, including the Eastern Wood-Pewee and Red-eyed Vireo.

Deciduous and mixed forest. Forages low and on the ground for insects, spiders, earthworms, and snails and in shrubs, vines, and trees for berries. Nest usually placed below 20 feet on tree branch or fork, and is a mud-sealed cup of grasses, forbs, and leaves.

Look for them at Calvert Cliffs State Park and Flag Ponds Nature Park, MD, and at Beaverdam Park (north entrance), VA. Fairly common nester in Upper and mid-Bay mid-April to early October; uncommon in Lower Bay region.

Song varies but always sounds flute-like: *too-too ... teeoh Eeeoo EEE*. Call loud, terse *pit-wit-wit*.

See Hermit Thrush (page 242).

Adult.
Flat gray-brown above. Adult males usually noticeably darker on head. Orange below, with white vent. Broken white goggles.

Juvenile.
Pale buff orange and whitish below with dark spots.

AMERICAN ROBIN

Turdus migratorius Length: 10" / Wingspan: 17"

One of the Bay's most familiar and plentiful songbirds. It's estimated that there are 380 million American Robins—one for each person living in the United States and Canada!

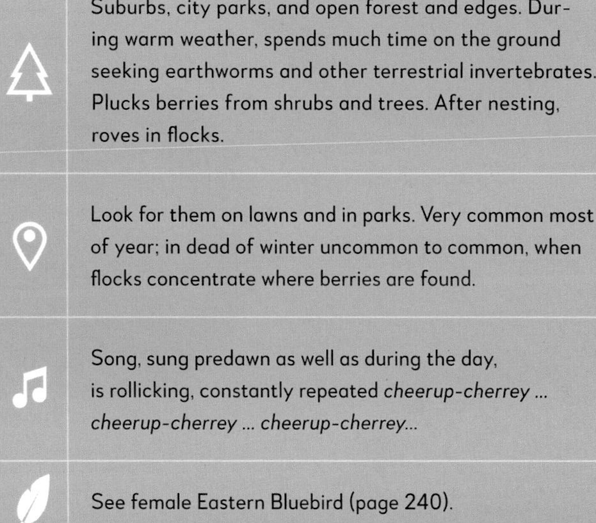

Suburbs, city parks, and open forest and edges. During warm weather, spends much time on the ground seeking earthworms and other terrestrial invertebrates. Plucks berries from shrubs and trees. After nesting, roves in flocks.

Look for them on lawns and in parks. Very common most of year; in dead of winter uncommon to common, when flocks concentrate where berries are found.

Song, sung predawn as well as during the day, is rollicking, constantly repeated *cheerup-cherrey ... cheerup-cherrey ... cheerup-cherrey...*

See female Eastern Bluebird (page 240).

Adult male.
Dull red head and breast. Heavily streaked with brown below. Blunt bill.

Adult female.
Unmarked brown head. Heavily streaked with brown below. Blunt bill.

Adult male (top) and female (bottom) Purple Finch.
Male is wine-colored on head, back, breast, wings, and sides. Female has striped head, with dark brown crown, mask, and malar stripe, and is heavily streaked in brown below. Compared with House Finch, tail shorter and notched.

HOUSE FINCH

Haemorhous mexicanus Length: 6" / Wingspan: 10"

This well-named songbird nests in hanging baskets, ornamental conifers, and even sometimes on apartment window ledges. Smaller and more blunt-billed than a sparrow, this now-widespread bird is not native to the Chesapeake Bay. Its ancestors were released cage birds hailing from the western United States or Mexico.

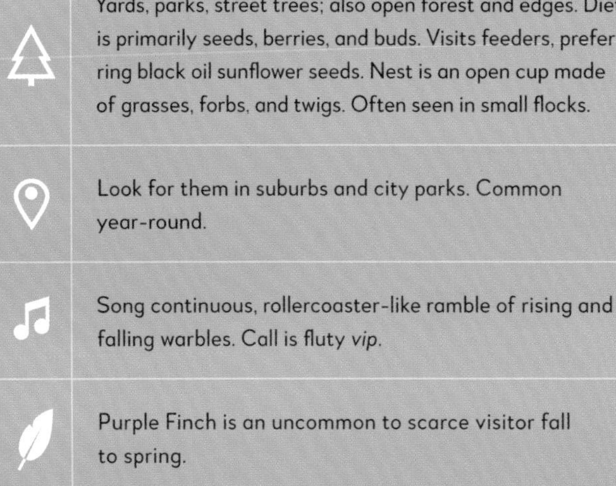

Yards, parks, street trees; also open forest and edges. Diet is primarily seeds, berries, and buds. Visits feeders, preferring black oil sunflower seeds. Nest is an open cup made of grasses, forbs, and twigs. Often seen in small flocks.

Look for them in suburbs and city parks. Common year-round.

Song continuous, rollercoaster-like ramble of rising and falling warbles. Call is fluty *vip*.

Purple Finch is an uncommon to scarce visitor fall to spring.

Breeding male.
Bright yellow with black fore-crown, wings, and tail. Female breeding plumage (not shown) similar to nonbreeding but with pale yellow on body.

Nonbreeding.
Olive body with pale yellowish head and wingbars. White vent. Dark wings and bill. Nonbreeding male shows more yellow on face, throat, and shoulder.

Adult Pine Siskin.
Streaks all over, with yellow blaze on wings and sides of tail. Much more pointed bill than in "red" finches.

AMERICAN GOLDFINCH

Spinus tristis Length: 5" / Wingspan: 9"

The canary-yellow male goldfinch is one of the Bay's most dazzling birds. Males molt into striking colors by April, changing back to drab olive in September. Goldfinches are among the last songbirds to nest, usually starting in July.

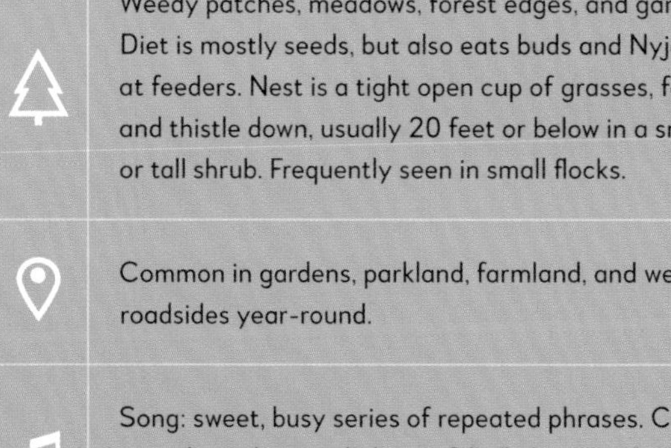

Weedy patches, meadows, forest edges, and gardens. Diet is mostly seeds, but also eats buds and Nyjer seed at feeders. Nest is a tight open cup of grasses, forbs, and thistle down, usually 20 feet or below in a small tree or tall shrub. Frequently seen in small flocks.

Common in gardens, parkland, farmland, and weedy roadsides year-round.

Song: sweet, busy series of repeated phrases. Call: dipping then whining *chuh-uree*? In flight: *per-chick-aree ... per-chick-aree ... per-chick-aree*.

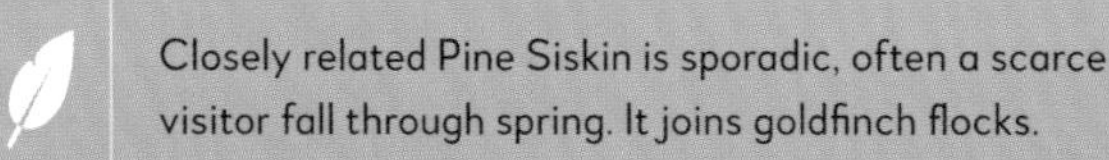

Closely related Pine Siskin is sporadic, often a scarce visitor fall through spring. It joins goldfinch flocks.

Breeding male.
Chestnut hindneck, black throat and breast, and gray crown.

Female.
Unmarked below and just one diffuse stripe on head. Thick, horn-colored bill.

HOUSE SPARROW

Passer domesticus Length: 6.25" / Wingspan: 9.5"

This introduced Eurasian species lives alongside people. It is not related to the Bay's other sparrows. Like other wild birds, House Sparrows face many dangers yet some individuals live surprisingly long lives. This species' longevity record in the wild is over 13 years.

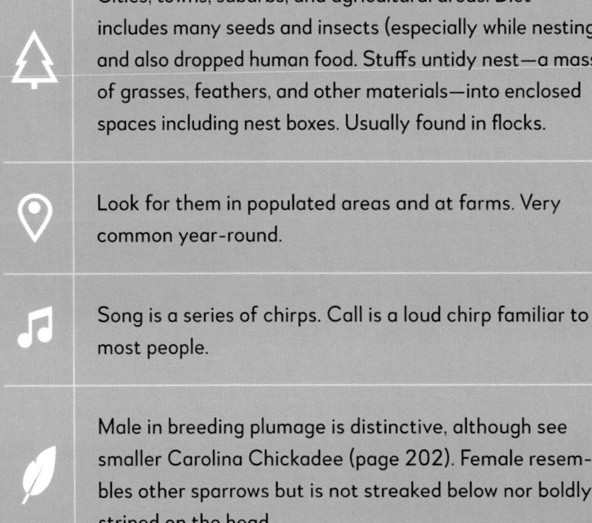

Cities, towns, suburbs, and agricultural areas. Diet includes many seeds and insects (especially while nesting), and also dropped human food. Stuffs untidy nest—a mass of grasses, feathers, and other materials—into enclosed spaces including nest boxes. Usually found in flocks.

Look for them in populated areas and at farms. Very common year-round.

Song is a series of chirps. Call is a loud chirp familiar to most people.

Male in breeding plumage is distinctive, although see smaller Carolina Chickadee (page 202). Female resembles other sparrows but is not streaked below nor boldly striped on the head.

Breeding adult.
Bright rust cap, with bold white eyebrow and thin black stripe through eye. Unmarked gray below.

Nonbreeding adult.
Dingy version of spring head pattern with little to no rust (and pale line down middle of crown). Gray breast and collar.

Adult Field Sparrow.
All-pink-orange bill. Rust on crown and behind eye. Lacks black or white head stripes.

CHIPPING SPARROW

Spizella passerina

Length: 5.5" / Wingspan: 8.5"

This jaunty little sparrow proclaims its territory all day long from atop trees overlooking grassy expanses. Adults have bold head patterns from late March to August.

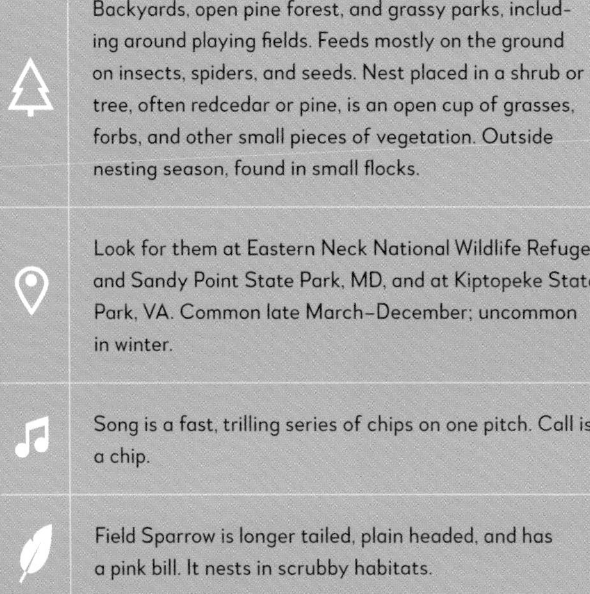

Backyards, open pine forest, and grassy parks, including around playing fields. Feeds mostly on the ground on insects, spiders, and seeds. Nest placed in a shrub or tree, often redcedar or pine, is an open cup of grasses, forbs, and other small pieces of vegetation. Outside nesting season, found in small flocks.

Look for them at Eastern Neck National Wildlife Refuge and Sandy Point State Park, MD, and at Kiptopeke State Park, VA. Common late March–December; uncommon in winter.

Song is a fast, trilling series of chips on one pitch. Call is a chip.

Field Sparrow is longer tailed, plain headed, and has a pink bill. It nests in scrubby habitats.

White-striped adult.
White eyebrow between thin black stripes. White throat stands out, surrounded by gray. Gray bill.

Tan striped/juvenile.
Tan eyebrow between blackish stripes. Whitish throat stands out, but not as clearly bordered as in white-striped birds. Gray bill.

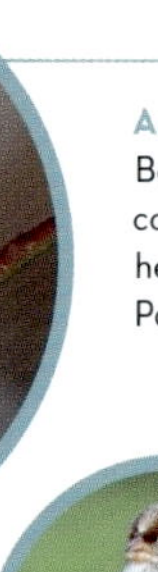

Adult White-crowned Sparrow.
Bold black-and-white head pattern contrasts with otherwise gray head and underparts. Pinkish bill. Pale throat lacks clear borders.

Juvenile White-crowned Sparrow.
Brown head stripes on otherwise grayish head and gray underparts. Pinkish bill.

WHITE-THROATED SPARROW

Zonotrichia albicollis Length: 6.75" / Wingspan: 9"

This plentiful sparrow comes in two forms—tan striped and white striped. One of the Bay region's most common wintering songbirds, its flocks seem to haunt every brushy woodland and forest edge. As if to remind observers that it's just visiting, it sings from time to time, a sweet *oh sweet Canada, Canada.*

Open forest, woodland edges, and brushy places. Spends a lot of time feeding on the ground, seeking seeds and invertebrates, and also some berries.

Watch for it in backyards, city parks, and any forested area. Very common October–May.

In addition to song noted above, listen for distinctive call: *pink, pink, pink.*

White-crowned Sparrow is uncommon to scarce fall to early spring in hedgy farm country.

Adult.
Cloudy dark grayish with yellow spot between eye and bill. Long dark gray bill.

Adult Saltmarsh Sparrow.
Buffy head with gray ear patch and nape. Thin, crisp breast streaks on whitish underparts. White stripes on back. Long yellowish bill.

Adult Nelson's Sparrow.
Dull orangish head and breast with clouded, not crisp, streaks below. Gray is more diffuse on head, and back stripes duller.

SEASIDE SPARROW

Ammospiza maritima Length: 6" / Wingspan: 7.5"

This dark, long-billed sparrow skulks in tidal marshes and is most visible when males sing in spring and summer. Its range on the Bay has contracted southward in recent decades, likely due to loss of low marshland.

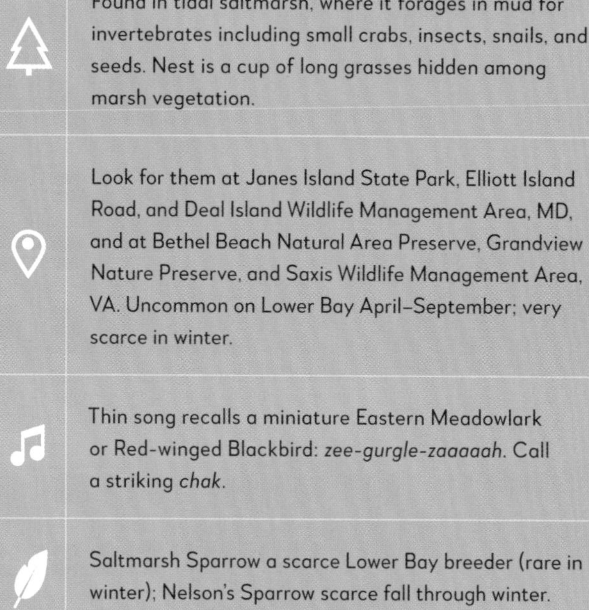

Found in tidal saltmarsh, where it forages in mud for invertebrates including small crabs, insects, snails, and seeds. Nest is a cup of long grasses hidden among marsh vegetation.

Look for them at Janes Island State Park, Elliott Island Road, and Deal Island Wildlife Management Area, MD, and at Bethel Beach Natural Area Preserve, Grandview Nature Preserve, and Saxis Wildlife Management Area, VA. Uncommon on Lower Bay April–September; very scarce in winter.

Thin song recalls a miniature Eastern Meadowlark or Red-winged Blackbird: *zee-gurgle-zaaaaah*. Call a striking *chak*.

Saltmarsh Sparrow a scarce Lower Bay breeder (rare in winter); Nelson's Sparrow scarce fall through winter.

Adult.
Triangle of spots: two prominent dark triangles frame the throat; below them sits a large central breast spot, just out of view on this bird. Long tail.

Adult Savannah Sparrow.
Yellowish between bill and eyes. Finer streaks below, with shorter, notched tail.

Adult Fox Sparrow.

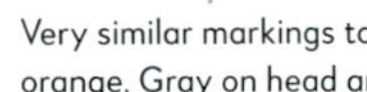

Very similar markings to Song but reddish-orange. Gray on head and collar, with yellow-orange bill. Reddish-orange tail.

Adult Lincoln's Sparrow.
Grayish head with light buffy wash on breast, sides, and malar (between throat and face). Thinner streaks on breast and back than on Song. Crown may appear pointed.

SONG SPARROW

Melospiza melodia Length: 6.3" / Wingspan: 8.25"

This melodious, streaky sparrow is a common backyard bird, singing in small trees and shrubs and lurking in gardens and at the edges of lawns.

Yards, parks, meadows, wetland edges, and damp, weedy, brush-lined drainage ditches. Forages on the ground and low in shrubs for seeds, insects, and berries. Nest is an open grassy cup, placed low and well concealed in shrubs, grasses, or forbs.

Watch for them in shrubby suburban yards and in most of the parks mentioned in this book. Common year-round, though on Lower Bay most common in winter.

Engaging song has three parts: slow, short series; ringing trill; and one- or two-note finish. Most common call is emphatic *kemp*.

See Swamp Sparrow (page 262). Savannah Sparrow fairly common migrant, uncommon breeder and wintering species. Fox Sparrow uncommon late fall through winter. Lincoln's Sparrow is scarce migrant.

Breeding adult male.
Rusty cap and wings. Lacks wingbars. Breast and much of head are gray. Contrasting white throat. Buffy flanks.

Nonbreeding.
Rust wings without wingbars. Buffy flanks. Grayish on head and collar. Dark malar frames pale throat. Gray breast with vague streaking.

SWAMP SPARROW

Melospiza georgiana Length: 5.75" / Wingspan: 7.25"

The Swamp Sparrow is the Song Sparrow's grayish-headed, rusty-winged cousin. During migration and winter, the two species are often found together.

Marshes, wetland edges, vegetated drainage ponds and ditches. Forages on damp ground or mud, seeking insects, spiders, and seeds. Nest is a cup, loosely woven outside, tightly inside, made of grasses and other plant stalks and usually placed just above water or ground.

Watch for them at Marshy Point Nature Center and Blackwater National Wildlife Refuge, MD, and at Dameron Marsh Natural Area Preserve and Kiptopeke State Park, VA. Fairly common October–May. A very local nester in some Coastal Plain marshes.

Song slow series of chips (of one or two syllables), slower and in shorter series than Chipping Sparrow. Call a hearty *pip*.

See Song Sparrow (page 260) and White-throated Sparrow (page 256).

Adult male.
Black head, back, and wings and rufous sides. White belly, wing square, and tail corners. Red eye.

Adult female.
Brown head, back, and wings and rufous sides. White belly, wing square, and tail corners. Red eye.

Male Dark-eyed Junco.
Dark slate above with contrasting white belly. Whitish bill. White outer tail feathers. Female similar but lighter gray, with some brownish tones.

EASTERN TOWHEE

Pipilo erythrophthalmus Length: 7.5" / Wingspan: 10.5"

This large, colorful sparrow scoots back and forth, stirring up the leaf litter. Though their head, wing, and back colors differ, females and males otherwise share the same color scheme—a “creamsicle” combo of orange and white below, with white wing squares and tail corners.

Dense undergrowth in open forest or edge. Eats berries, invertebrates, and seeds. Nest is an open cup of grasses, twigs, and forbs, located on the ground or low in a shrub.

Look for them at Franklin Point State Park, Marshy Point Nature Center, and Eastern Neck National Wildlife Refuge, MD, and at First Landing State Park and Eastern Shore of Virginia National Wildlife Refuge, VA. Fairly common year-round.

Song distinctive *drink-your-tea*. *She-wink* or *tow-weeh* call given year-round.

Smaller Dark-eyed Junco, common October–April, has flashy white outer tail feathers; the towhee has white tail corners.

Adult.
Yellow below, black V-shaped breast band, heavy side streaking. Striped head and long, pointy bill. Long legs.

Adult male Dickcissel.
Rusty shoulder. Mostly yellow eyebrow, malar, and breast. Sparrow-like shape. No streaking below. Female drab, resembling female House Sparrow but with rusty shoulder, dark malar stripe, and yellowish tones.

EASTERN MEADOWLARK

Sturnella magna Length: 9.5" / Wingspan: 14"

Facing you, this bird flashes bold omelet-yellow, emblazoned with a black V. Facing away, it blends with its earthy surroundings thanks to its scaled, striped, and straw-colored back and wings.

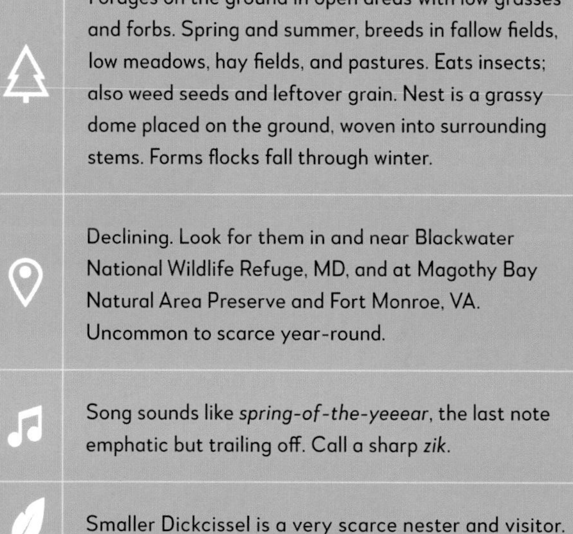

Forages on the ground in open areas with low grasses and forbs. Spring and summer, breeds in fallow fields, low meadows, hay fields, and pastures. Eats insects; also weed seeds and leftover grain. Nest is a grassy dome placed on the ground, woven into surrounding stems. Forms flocks fall through winter.

Declining. Look for them in and near Blackwater National Wildlife Refuge, MD, and at Magothy Bay Natural Area Preserve and Fort Monroe, VA. Uncommon to scarce year-round.

Song sounds like *spring-of-the-yeeear*, the last note emphatic but trailing off. Call a sharp *zik*.

Smaller Dickcissel is a very scarce nester and visitor.

Adult male.
Burnt-orange body with black head, back, and tail.

Adult female.
Dull yellow with gray wings and whitish wingbars. Immature male almost identical but has black throat.

Adult male Baltimore Oriole.
Dazzling citrus-orange with black head, back, and tail. Orange tail corners.

Adult female Baltimore Oriole.
Orangey with variable blackish mottling on head and back.

ORCHARD ORIOLE

Icterus spurius Length: 7.25" / Wingspan: 9.5"

North America's smallest oriole often "hides" in plain sight, dark males singing within view but in leafy treetops. They often nest near Eastern Kingbirds, likely benefiting from the belligerent birds' vigilance against trespassers.

Marsh and forest edges, and in parks, suburbs, and brushy areas dotted with trees. Gleans insects; also consumes berries and nectar. The ball-shaped nest, made of interwoven grasses, hangs from a branch fork.

Look for them at Eastern Neck National Wildlife Refuge, MD, and at Kiptopeke State Park and Beaverdam Park (north entrance), VA. Common late April–August.

Sings ramble of sweet, twangy, and sharp notes. Calls: sweet *cheeo* and scolding *pididit*.

Baltimore Oriole nests in Upper Bay, often in same areas as Orchard, and is common migrant. In winter, a few loiter at feeders in southeastern Virginia. See also female Summer Tanager (page 292).

Adult male.
All black except for red shoulder patch with yellow border.

Adult female.
Very streaky; resembles blackbird-shaped sparrow. Light buff on head. Pointy bill.

RED-WINGED BLACKBIRD

Agelaius phoeniceus Length: 8.75" / Wingspan: 13"

Spring's promise hangs in the air when the male Red-winged Blackbird's *conkereee!* begins echoing across marshes and fields. Males spend most of their day singing and defending small territories—even mobbing trespassing eagles and herons.

Forages in marshes, meadows, fallow fields, and pastures, eating grains, seeds, and insects on the ground and in vegetation. Nest is an open cup of vegetation strips, woven around reed or cattail stems or a vertical tree or shrub trunk. Outside breeding season, forms large flocks, at times mingling with other blackbirds and starlings.

Look for them in any wetland, including at Sandy Point State Park and Blackwater National Wildlife Refuge, MD, and at New Point Comfort Natural Area Preserve, VA. Common year-round.

Song clear *konkereeee!* Call is flat *check*. Alarm calls include loud *seeer!*

Streaky females and immatures can be confused for large sparrows.

Adult male.
Glossy black body and contrasting brown head. Compared with region's other blackbirds, this bird has a shorter tail and shorter, thicker bill.

Adult female.
Brown with no wingbars or other striking features. Pale throat. Bill thicker than a sparrow's and shorter than those of other blackbirds.

BROWN-HEADED COWBIRD

Molothrus ater

Length: 7.5" / Wingspan: 12"

Female cowbirds lay their eggs in other birds' nests, leaving hosts—including warblers, gnatcatchers, Wood Thrushes, and Song Sparrows—to raise their robust young to the detriment of their own.

Forages in farm fields and on lawns; females skulk in forest foliage, watching for nesting songbirds. Often seen in flocks with other blackbirds.

Look for them in farmland, suburbs, and forest edges. Common spring through fall; uncommon in winter.

Male's song has three or four bubbling notes followed by rising high note, like *bump-a-lump-oh-see*. Calls: high-pitched *see-ee* and short but emphatic rattle.

Female Blue Grosbeak has thicker bill and dull orange wing bars. (See Indigo Bunting, page 296, for photo.) See also juvenile European Starling (page 238).

Adult male.
Long, keel-shaped tail and long, thick bill. Piercing yellow eye. Metallic purplish, green, blue, and bronze tones. Female is similar but plumage less iridescent.

Female Boat-tailed Grackle.
Saltmarsh habitat. Buffy-brown head and underparts and yellow eye. Long tail, but not as long as male's. Male like a larger, stretched-out version of Common.

Nonbreeding male Rusty Blackbird.
Favors swamps. Regular-length tail is not keeled. Thinner bill. Rust color on head and wings. Female (not shown) lighter and browner. Pale eye. In spring, males are dark and glossy, recalling grackles.

COMMON GRACKLE

Quiscalus quiscula Length: 12.5" / Wingspan: 17"

Male grackles start courting females in late winter, puffing out their iridescent plumage and singing. This adaptable blackbird dominates many a backyard, strutting over the grass and nesting in conifers, often near other pairs.

Suburbs, city parks, woodland edges, and swampy areas. Forages on the ground, and to a lesser degree in shrubs and trees. Eats grains, fruits, and insects. Flocks from late summer through winter.

Look for them in city parks and gardens and in many other semiopen habitats. Very common much of year; common in late fall and winter, when large flocks concentrate in agricultural areas.

Rusty-hinge-like *koh-reek*, often sung after puffing up. Call is loud *chuk*.

Rusty Blackbird is uncommon in swamps October–April. Larger Boat-tailed Grackle is restricted to tidal saltmarshes of the Lower Bay.

Adult.
Thrush-like coloration: olive-brown above and spotted below. White eyering. Black-bordered orange crown.

Adult Northern Waterthrush.
Whitish eyebrow stripe tapers at back of head. Fine streaks at throat bottom. Often has light yellowish wash below.

Adult Louisiana Waterthrush.
White eyebrow stripe ends wide. Clear white throat bottom. Often shows buffy flanks.

OVENBIRD

Seiurus aurocapilla Length: 6" / Wingspan: 9.5"

Like a mini thrush with a colorful crown, the Ovenbird is distinctive, if you can spot it walking quietly across the forest floor. It's far easier, though, to detect this bird by its distinctive song.

Forages within deciduous and mixed forest, searching leaf litter for insects, spiders, snails, and earthworms. The nest, placed on the ground, is a dome made of leaves, stems, and bark strips, with a side entrance.

Look for them at Blackwater National Wildlife Refuge and Calvert Cliffs State Park, MD, and at Beaverdam Park (north entrance) and York River State Park, VA. Fairly common to uncommon nester in large forest tracts, mid-April to early October.

Song's notes grow louder but stay on same plane: *Teacher TEACHER TEACHER TEACHER.*

Northern Waterthrush a common migrant, particularly in spring. Louisiana Waterthrush a fairly common breeder from late March to mid-August.

Breeding male.
Zebra striped, with striped head and black throat and ear patch. Female and immature lack black throat and ear patch; nonbreeding male lacks black throat.

Breeding male Blackpoll Warbler.
Black cap and white cheek. Gray back with black streaks. (Lacks bold head pattern in fall.)

Breeding female Blackpoll Warbler.
Female plumage varies, sometimes resembling faded version of breeding male (as shown). Streaky, grayish crown. Dark surrounds pale cheek. Yellow legs.

BLACK-AND-WHITE WARBLER

Mniotilta varia Length: 5.25" / Wingspan: 8.25"

This zebra-striped warbler clambers over tree trunks and branches, acting more like a nuthatch than a warbler.

Forages on tree trunks, probing and gleaning bark and foliage for insect prey. Found in deciduous and mixed forests, and edges during migration. Nest, placed on the forest floor, often in a recess next to a tree or bush, is an open cup crafted of leaves, grasses, bark strips, and pine needles.

Look for them at Calvert Cliffs State Park and Flag Ponds Nature Park, MD, and at York River State Park and Beaverdam Park (north entrance), VA. Common migrant and uncommon, local nester, present April–October.

Song high-pitched string of two syllables, like *weesy weesy weesy weesy weesy*. Reminds some of a rolling, squeaky wheel.

Blackpoll Warbler a common migrant in May and again in September and October.

Adult male.
Black mask fringed with white above. Bright yellow throat and breast.

Adult female.
Plain gray-olive head contrasted by yellow throat. Immature similar but immature male shows traces of black on face.

Adult male Prairie Warbler.
Bright yellow with distinctive face pattern and black side streaks. Some rust color on back. Female and immature have faint version of face pattern.

Adult Yellow-breasted Chat.
Much larger and longer tailed, with white goggles and mustache contrasting with bright yellow breast and dark olive upperparts.

COMMON YELLOWTHROAT

Geothlypis trichas Length: 5" / Wingspan: 6.75"

Unlike most warblers, the yellowthroat won't strain your neck. The masked male sings low in bushes and young trees in open, non-forest habitats. Wren-like in habit, this cock-tailed songbird is among the Bay's most common warblers.

Low, moist terrain including wetland edges and meadows. Creeps around in the shadows, seeking insects and spiders. Nest, a loose cup of grasses and other vegetation, is placed on or near the ground, hidden amid vegetation.

Look for them at Marshy Point Nature Center and Eastern Neck National Wildlife Refuge, MD, and at Grandview Nature Preserve and Sandy Bottom Nature Park, VA. Common from mid-April through October; scarce in winter on Lower Bay.

Song a loud *wichity-wichity-wichity*. Call a somewhat burry *chik*.

Prairie Warbler and Yellow-breasted Chat also nest in thickety habitats, though usually not near water.

Adult male.
Satiny black with orange on sides, wings, and tail. White belly.

Female.
Flashes yellow at tail base. Yellow wing blaze and sides. Immature similar.

AMERICAN REDSTART

Setophaga ruticilla Length: 5.25" / Wingspan: 7.75"

While working the foliage, this flashy warbler startles prey into view by fanning its tail feathers. In coloration, adult males resemble miniature orioles, setting them apart from other warblers.

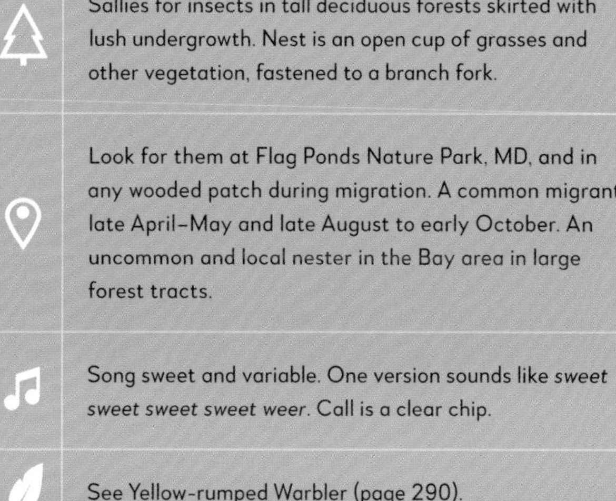

Sallies for insects in tall deciduous forests skirted with lush undergrowth. Nest is an open cup of grasses and other vegetation, fastened to a branch fork.

Look for them at Flag Ponds Nature Park, MD, and in any wooded patch during migration. A common migrant late April–May and late August to early October. An uncommon and local nester in the Bay area in large forest tracts.

Song sweet and variable. One version sounds like *sweet sweet sweet sweet weer*. Call is a clear chip.

See Yellow-rumped Warbler (page 290).

Adult male.
Blue head and wings, mustard-colored back patch. Yellow throat and breast with bronze breast band. White arcs above and below eye. Female similar but duller, with bronzy band less defined.

NORTHERN PARULA

Setophaga americana Length: 4.5" / Wingspan: 7"

Zipping around high in the canopy, this tiny warbler is often heard but is tough to find. When glimpsed well, it is a treat for the eyes with its blue head, white eye crescents, and yellow-and-orange breast.

Found in mature swamp forest and wooded stream and river banks, gleaning leaves and hovering to catch insects and spiders. Nest is a suspended pouch of woven plant materials, usually built within a clump of vegetation or flood-deposited debris.

Look for them at Calvert Cliffs State Park and Flag Ponds Nature Park, MD, and at York River and First Landing State Parks, VA. Common from mid-April well into October. Most widespread as a nester on the Western Shore.

Two commonly heard buzzy songs: *zzzzzzzz-zeee-up!* and *wees-wees-wees-zee-zee-zee*. Call a clear chip.

When seen well, this warbler is distinctive, but see Blue-gray Gnatcatcher (page 226).

Adult male.
All yellow (including wingbars) with vivid orange streaks below.

Adult female.
All somewhat dull yellow.

Adult male Prothonotary Warbler.
Gold with gray wings and white undertail. Female similar but not as vividly colored.

YELLOW WARBLER

Setophaga petechia Length: 5" / Wingspan: 8"

This vivid little bird has declined as a Bay-region breeder, likely due to loss of young-forest habitats.

Forages in brushy areas with scattered trees, often by water. Gleans, flycatches, and hovers, grabbing caterpillars and other invertebrates. Nest is an open cup of grasses, forbs, and bark strips built in a shrub or small tree.

Look for them at Eastern Neck National Wildlife Refuge and Swan Harbor Farm Park, MD, and at Eastern Shore of Virginia National Wildlife Refuge, VA (migration). Common migrant, especially late April–May. Nests in some areas of the Upper Bay; patchy and declining elsewhere.

Song often sounds like *Sweet-sweet-sweet-sweet, I'm so sweet*. Call a rich chip.

Prothonotary Warbler nests locally in bottomland swamps and riverine forests such as Pocomoke River, MD, and First Landing State Park, VA.

Adult male.
Dull yellow head, back, and breast, often with some blurry streaks below. Whitish on belly and undertail. White wingbars. Female has slightly duller coloration.

Adult Yellow-throated Warbler.
Bright yellow throat framed with black. Black face fringed by white. White sides with bold black streaks.

PINE WARBLER

Setophaga pinus Length: 5.5" / Wingspan: 8.75"

This yellowy songbird is the only warbler to winter almost entirely within the United States, including along the Lower Bay.

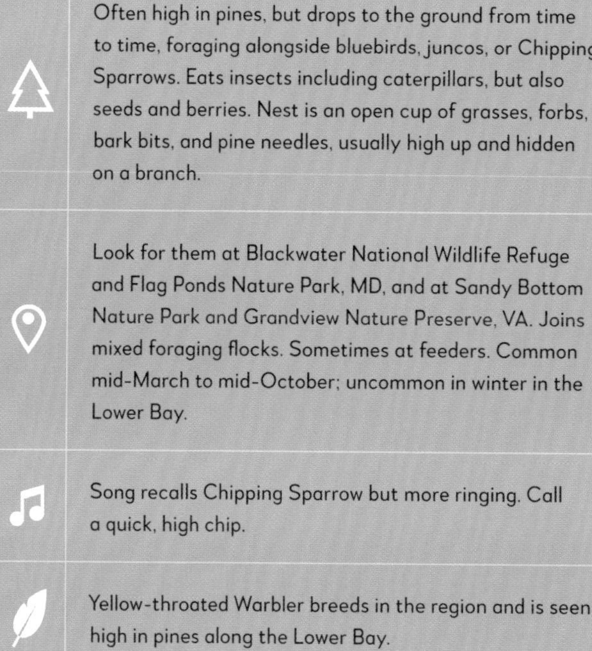

Often high in pines, but drops to the ground from time to time, foraging alongside bluebirds, juncos, or Chipping Sparrows. Eats insects including caterpillars, but also seeds and berries. Nest is an open cup of grasses, forbs, bark bits, and pine needles, usually high up and hidden on a branch.

Look for them at Blackwater National Wildlife Refuge and Flag Ponds Nature Park, MD, and at Sandy Bottom Nature Park and Grandview Nature Preserve, VA. Joins mixed foraging flocks. Sometimes at feeders. Common mid-March to mid-October; uncommon in winter in the Lower Bay.

Song recalls Chipping Sparrow but more ringing. Call a quick, high chip.

Yellow-throated Warbler breeds in the region and is seen high in pines along the Lower Bay.

Nonbreeding. Prominent yellow rump and sides. Washed in tan-olive and lightly streaked, with a whitish throat. Whitish wingbars.

Breeding adult male. Bold yellow side patch and rump; yellowish crown. Heavy black streaking across breast and on sides. Black mask contrasts with white throat. Breeding female's plumage similar but subdued, and she lacks yellow crown patch.

Nonbreeding Palm Warbler. Pale yellow undertail. Otherwise, brownish gray, with no wingbars. Some have yellowish eyebrow and underparts in addition to undertail. Pumps tail.

YELLOW-RUMPED WARBLER

Setophaga coronata Length: 5.5" / Wingspan: 9.25"

Late fall through winter, you should encounter chipping flocks of this cooperative songbird, the Bay's most commonly seen warbler. The "yellow-rump" is the standard from which other warblers can be separated. Formerly called Myrtle Warbler for its affinity for fall and winter wax myrtle (bayberry) berries.

Forages low and high in trees and tall shrubs in wide range of habitats. Eats insects and berries. Often associates with other foraging species.

Found in parks, at forest edges, and in thickets and tall shrubs dotting wetlands. In winter, the only warbler very common on the Lower Bay and fairly common on the Upper Bay. Widespread during migration. Does not nest in Bay region.

Song lazing, sweet series or two of notes ending without flourish. Call is distinctive loud, flat chip.

Palm Warbler is early spring migrant and late, lingering fall migrant; scarce in winter.

Adult male.
Rose colored, including on wings. Tanager bill (thick and long).

Adult female.
Wings match body color (not blackish as in female and nonbreeding male Scarlet). Often rich olive-yellow as shown, but coloration varies. Tanager bill (thick and long). Some females and molting immature males have orange or red patches.

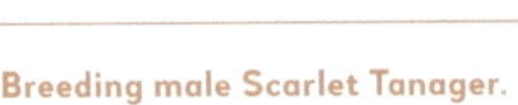

Breeding male Scarlet Tanager.
Dazzling scarlet with jet-black wings and tail. Nonbreeding birds resemble female but with more black on wings.

Adult female Scarlet Tanager.
Greenish-yellow with blackish wings and tail. Tanager bill (thick and long).

SUMMER TANAGER

Piranga rubra

Length: 7.75" / Wingspan: 12"

Of the three all-red male songbirds found in the Bay region, this one is the closest to pinkish-red in color.

Mixed forests, often including pines, oaks, and hickories. Forages mid-level and higher in trees, snapping up wasps, bees, and other insects. Eats some berries. Nest is a shallow cup of grasses, forbs, bark, and leaves on a horizontal tree branch. Usually seen singly or in pairs.

Look for them at Calvert Cliffs State Park and Flag Ponds Nature Park, MD, and at Sandy Bottom Nature Park and Woodville Park, VA. Fairly common late April–September, mostly on the mid- to Lower Bay.

Sweet song recalls American Robin. Call distinctive, rapid *tick-kuk* or *ticky tucky tuck*.

See Northern Cardinal (page 294). Scarlet Tanager breeds around the Bay, especially in mid- and Upper Bay forests; also common in migration.

Adult male.
All red and crested, with black face and thick, triangular orange-red bill.

Adult female.
Mostly warm tan, with reddish wings, tail, and crest, and orange-red bill. Whitish belly.

Adult male Rose-breasted Grosbeak.
Bright red triangular breast patch, black head, and very thick whitish bill.

Adult female/immature Rose-breasted Grosbeak.
Dark mask on striped head. Very thick bill. Compare with female Purple Finch.

NORTHERN CARDINAL

Cardinalis cardinalis Length: 8.75" / Wingspan: 12"

Cardinal pairs stay together year-round, and they don't migrate. Unlike most songbirds, females sing, duetting with their mates from time to time. Virginia's state bird, this colorful species is often underappreciated because it's seen so often.

Wide variety of habitats with shrubs and trees, including backyards. Uses its thick bill to crack open seed pods and sunflower seeds. Also plucks and eats berries and eats insects, spiders, and other invertebrates. Loosely crafted nest of twigs, forb stems, and bark is hidden in a large shrub or young tree.

Look for them in any garden or park. Very common year-round.

Song clear, sweet *wit wit wit chew chew chew chew chew chew* or similar. Call a piercing chip.

See Summer Tanager (page 292). The related Rose-breasted Grosbeak passes through in migration.

Breeding adult male.
All bright blue.
Sparrow-like bill.

Adult female.
Understated, plain and tan, with unmarked head and faint tan wingbars. Sparrow-like bill. Bluish on tail.

Adult male Blue Grosbeak.
Blue with rusty wingbars and cardinal-like bill.

Adult female Blue Grosbeak.
Plain, with rusty shoulder and cardinal-like bill.

INDIGO BUNTING

Passerina cyanea Length: 5.5" / Wingspan: 8"

Among the region's most dazzling songbirds, male Indigo Buntings sing all day long from treetops and wires, yet many people don't notice them. Up high and in strong sunlight or overcast, these birds could be passed off as small, dark sparrows.

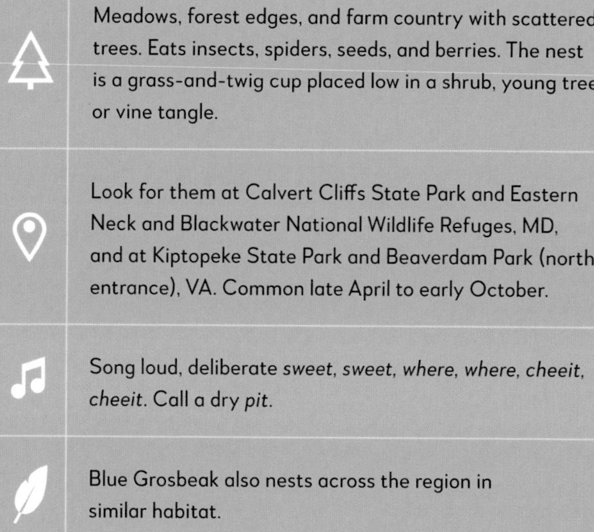

Meadows, forest edges, and farm country with scattered trees. Eats insects, spiders, seeds, and berries. The nest is a grass-and-twig cup placed low in a shrub, young tree, or vine tangle.

Look for them at Calvert Cliffs State Park and Eastern Neck and Blackwater National Wildlife Refuges, MD, and at Kiptopeke State Park and Beaverdam Park (north entrance), VA. Common late April to early October.

Song loud, deliberate *sweet, sweet, where, where, cheeit, cheeit*. Call a dry *pit*.

Blue Grosbeak also nests across the region in similar habitat.

ACCESSIBLE BIRDING SITES ALONG THE CHESAPEAKE BAY

Listed below are a few of the top birding spots with accessibility. Before visiting, research your particular needs to see if these sites work for you, and try to contact your targeted sites before you go, since facilities might be subject to change.

MARYLAND

Blackwater National Wildlife Refuge

The visitor center's second floor is reached by a wheelchair-accessible elevator and has a birder's observatory. The Marsh Edge Trail is a fully accessible paved trail that is a third of a mile long. Some of the best birding can be done around the visitor center and along the four-mile wildlife drive, which can be covered by car, on foot, or by bike. Phone 410-228-2677.

Eastern Neck National Wildlife Refuge

The Tidal Marsh Trail, behind the visitor center, is an accessible boardwalk through a meadow to a photo blind on the Chester River. The Tubby Cove Boardwalk Trail is accessible as well, though visitors should take care on the wooden boardwalk.

Point Lookout State Park

Many of the top viewpoints can be reached by car and seen from or near parking areas. Restrooms are ADA accessible.

Sandy Point State Park

Much of the park and its facilities are ADA accessible.

VIRGINIA

Eastern Shore of Virginia National Wildlife Refuge

The visitor center and parts of the Butterfly Trail are wheelchair accessible.

First Landing State Park

The Cape Henry Trail is wheelchair accessible, as are the Chesapeake Bay Center and Trail Center. Four campgrounds have accessible restrooms and showers. A special beach-access wheelchair is available. Phone 757-412-2320.

Holly Point Nature Park

This site is home of the Deltaville Maritime Museum and has wide pathways, picnic areas, and gardens and woodland edges along the Bay.

Kiptopeke State Park

The hawk migration observation area is ADA accessible, as is much of the fishing pier. A beach wheelchair is available, as are other accessible amenities.

RECOMMENDED RESOURCES

Site Guides

Birder's Guide to Maryland & DC / birdersguidemddc.org/
Birding in the Heart of Chesapeake Country: Trail Guide, Dorchester County, Maryland / dnr.maryland.gov/boating/documents/dor_birdingbrochure.pdf
Virginia Bird & Wildlife Trail / dwr.virginia.gov/vbwt/

Birding and Conservation Organizations and Websites

Alliance for the Chesapeake Bay / allianceforthebay.org
American Bird Conservancy / abcbirds.org
American Birding Association / aba.org
Chesapeake Bay Foundation / cbf.org
Chesapeake Conservancy / chesapeakeconservancy.org
Cornell Lab of Ornithology / birds.cornell.edu
Maryland Biodiversity Project / marylandbiodiversity.com
Maryland Ornithological Society / mdbirds.org
National Audubon Society / audubon.org
Virginia Society of Ornithology / virginiabirds.org

Comprehensive Field Guides

National Geographic Field Guide to the Birds of the United States and Canada (eighth edition) by Ted Floyd
The Sibley Guide to Birds (second edition) by David Allen Sibley

TERNS OF PHRASE

We all know it but won't often say it: Bird names can sound funny. Many, such as eight found in this paragraph, provide perfect pun fodder that might inspire smiles or groans. Here's a swift exploration of how it's dunlin: If you're a plover of puns, read on, or you could just tern the page. Perhaps this paragraph seems hawkward. I hope this section will encourage you to keep heron and raven about bird puns. The question is, willet?

ACKNOWLEDGMENTS

Howard Youth

Writing a book like this is a rare privilege and a chance to share the fascination of birds and elevate the ongoing need for their conservation. My research drew on generations of field work and studies done by many others over the years. Regarding ever-changing bird distributions, updates are ongoing and now driven in good part by information that volunteers share on databases including eBird, which is managed by the Cornell Lab of Ornithology. eBird has been a game changer for birds and birding, as has been the Birds of the World database. A general thank-you to all of those researchers, birders, and reviewers who dedicate time and effort to share their observations on these and other platforms.

I'd like to thank all of my family and my friends for encouraging me while I was writing this book. Special thanks to birding and writing colleagues and pals Jim Nealon and Jon Selle, who regularly checked in on me and who reviewed drafts, providing great improvements. Jon also "ground-truthed" many of the noted birding locations with me, as did friend and coauthor Gemma Radko. Thanks also for the regular check-ins and encouragement from the Youth and Czochanski families, Al and Cathie Goltz, Tim Haering (who inspired the "Terns of Phrase" section), Amy Chang and Bob Young, and Joseph Pollack. And many thanks to my coauthor and friend Gemma Radko for joining me on this journey. Thanks to Gabriel Foley and Jordan Rutter for sparking the opportunity for me to talk to Timber Press about writing this book. We'd like to thank Ryan Harrington, Jacoba Lawson, Kathryn Juergens, Nick Dysinger, Sarah Crumb, and Kevin McConnell at Timber Press, and also copy editor extraordinaire Laura Whittemore at Kingbird Editorial.

Hugs to my parents, Ed and Helen, and my sisters, Gail and Leanne, for supporting my passion for birds from the early days, and also to my kids, Alessandra and Thomas, as well as my nephew and nieces, for their love and for sharing nature with me through the years. Most of all, I'd like to thank my best friend and wife, Marta, for her love, patience, and support, including listening to musings on bird minutiae for over 35 years!

Gemma Radko

I have been fascinated by birds for as long as I can remember. Many people helped foster my passion as I grew up, starting with my parents, who took me to my first Audubon Society meetings and bought me my first Golden field guide and pair of binoculars.

Birds and birding have since become a major part of my life, thanks to years of teaching ornithology and other bird-related subjects at Nature Forward and the friendship and support I've received from great friends and fellow bird enthusiasts (including Howard Youth!) that I have met through the Maryland Ornithological Society.

Thanks to Howard for giving me the opportunity to collaborate with him on this book, to my family, and to my husband Joseph for his unwavering support and love.

PHOTO AND ILLUSTRATION CREDITS

STEPHEN J. DAVIES, pages 52 top and bottom, 66, 70 top and middle, 74 top and middle, 76 bottom, 96 bottom, 126 bottom, 128 third from top, 138 top, 156 middle, 160 top, 168 middle, 180 middle, 200 bottom, 292 second from top, 294 second from top, 296 bottom.

Stephen began birding as a young boy in Wales in the early 1980s. He's since lived in upstate New York and San Francisco and has been a resident of the National Capital area since 2004. A student of nature, he has traveled to five continents in search of birds and other wildlife.

BILL HIGGINS, pages 2-3, 6, 19 left, 28 top, 50 top and middle, 52 middle, 54 bottom, 56, 62 bottom, 64 top, 68 top and middle, 70 bottom, 72 bottom, 76 top three, 78 bottom, 80 top and bottom, 84 top and bottom, 86 top and bottom, 88 bottom, 92 third from top, 94 top, 98 top three, 100 top, 104 top, 106 top, 108 top and bottom, 110 top three, 114 top, 116 top, 118 top and bottom, 120 bottom, 124 top and bottom, 126 top two, 128 bottom, 130 top and bottom, 132 bottom, 134 second from top, 138 second and third from top, 140 all, 142 top and third from top, 144 top and bottom, 146 top and middle, 148 both, 150 both, 152 both, 154 top and middle, 156 bottom, 158 top and middle, 162 top, 166 both, 170 top and bottom, 172 top, 174 bottom, 178 bottom, 182, 184, 186 bottom, 188, 208, 210 middle two photos and bottom, 214 top, 216 top, 218, 228 top, 230 top, 238 middle and bottom, 240 bottom, 246 bottom, 250 middle, 254 middle and bottom, 258 top, 262 top, 268 third from top, 270 top, 274 bottom, 278 all, 280 second from top, 290 middle and bottom, 292 bottom, 294 third from top, 296 second from top.

Bill started birding late but has been very active for almost twenty years now. His main angle is photography, and he is excited by the finds on each nature-site visit. He's spent many winters in Tucson and now primarily visits local spots in northern Virginia. A good walk, meditation, and a collection of images.

MARK R. JOHNSON, pages 15, 17, 21, 26 middle and bottom, 28 middle, 48-49, 54 top and middle, 58, 60, 62 top, 64 middle, 68 bottom, 72 top, 74 bottom, 78 top, 82 top and bottom, 88 top and middle, 90 bottom, 92 second from top and bottom, 94 middle and bottom, 96 top, 98 bottom, 102 top and bottom, 104 middle and bottom, 106 bottom, 110 bottom, 112 top, 114 middle and bottom, 116 bottom, 120 top, 126 third from top, 128 top two, 130 both middle, 134 top and bottom, 136 all, 138 bottom, 144 middle, 146 bottom, 160 bottom, 164 both, 168 bottom, 172 bottom, 174 middle, 176 top, 180 top and bottom, 186 top, 190 all, 192 all, 194 top and middle, 196 top, 198, 200 top, 202, 206 all, 210 top, 212 both, 214 bottom, 216 bottom, 226, 228 bottom, 232, 234, 236 both, 238 top, 240 top and middle, 242 middle and bottom, 246 top, 248 all,

250 top and bottom, 252 both, 256 top and third from top, 258 middle and bottom, 260 top and second from top, 262 bottom, 264 top and bottom, 266 top, 268 second from top, 270 bottom, 272 top, 274 all, 276 middle, 280 third from top and bottom, 282 bottom, 284, 286 all, 288 top, 290 top, 292 top, 294 top and bottom, 296 top and third from top.

Mark has been a lover of the great outdoors and enthusiastic observer of nature since early childhood. He didn't actually become a "birder" until much later in life and considers himself a birder first, then a photographer. Birding became a passionate hobby after retiring from a thirty-year career in public health—photography has just been a byproduct of his desire to document his observations, as well as a terrific identification learning tool.

JACQUES PITTELOUD, pages 5, 14, 18, 19 right, 25, 26 top, 28 bottom, 112 bottom, 122 top and bottom, 142 bottom, 154 bottom, 158 bottom, 162 bottom, 174 top, 176 bottom, 178 top and middle, 194 bottom, 196 bottom, 220 both, 222, 224, 230 bottom, 242 top, 244, 254 top, 256 second from top and bottom, 260 third from top and bottom, 264 middle, 266 bottom, 268 top, 272 bottom, 276 top and bottom, 280 top, 282 top, 288 bottom, 292 third from top.

Jacques started birdwatching half a century ago in his native mountains of Southern Switzerland. His diplomatic career allowed him to follow his passion on several continents and to publish his birding pictures in various books and publications in Europe and Africa.

LUCA PFEIFFER, *National Park Service, page 100 bottom*

ISTOCKPHOTO

CAROL HAMILTON, page 268 bottom

DSS IMAGES, page 168 top

IRVING A. GAFFNEY, page 156 top

MICHEL VIARD, page 132 top

NEIL BOWMAN, page 142 second from top

RANCHO RUNNER, page 92 top

STEVE BYLAND, page 204

TERRY KELLY, page 160 middle

TOMASZ ŚMIGLA, page 170 middle

WILLIAM KRUMPELMAN, page 90 top

WIRESTOCK, pags 134 third from top, 200 middle

WIKIMEDIA, CREATIVE COMMONS ATTRIBUTION 2.0 GENERIC LICENSE

ANDREW C, page 50 bottom

RUSS, page 200 middle

FAMILY SILHOUETTES

Geese, Swans & Ducks by Kristtaps/iStock.com
Grebes by Birchside/gograph.com
Loons by Rahul Kolgaonkar/pngitem.com
Coots & Rails by iDrawSilhouettes/creativefabrica.com
Turkeys based on a photo by Mark R. Johnson
Oystercatchers by ilyasov/iStock.com
Plovers by Birchside/gograph.com
Sandpiperss by Birchside/gograph.com
Gulls & Terns by Birchside/gograph.com

Gannets & Boobies based on a photo by Stephen J. Davies
Cormorants by piranjya/iStockPhoto.com
Pelican from pngitem.com
Herons & Egrets by Taras Adamovych/dreamstime.com
Ibises based on a photo by Mark R. Johnson
Vultures by iDrawSilhouettes/creativefabrica.com
Osprey by UfimtsevaV/iStock.com
Hawks & Eagles by vadimmmus/iStock.com
Falcons by PetrP/shutterstock.com
Owls based on a photo by Bill Higgins
Pigeons & Doves by DeCe_X/istockphoto.com
Cuckoos by based on a photo by Mark R. Johnson
Hummingbirds by mr.Timmi/shutterstock.com
Kingfishers by Birchside/gograph.com
Woodpeckers from pinclipart.com
Flycatchers by Bahau/shutterstock.com
Vireos based on a photo by VJAnderson / Wikimedia Commons (used under a CCA-SA 4.0 International license)
Jays & Crows by Vector SpMan/shutterstock.com
Chickadees & Titmice by SilhouetteGarden.com
Larks based on a photo by Mark R. Johnson
Swifts based on a photo by Bill Higgins
Swallows & Martins by Ivana Kontic/shutterstock.com
Kinglets based on an illustration by Viktoria Karpunina/shutterstock.com
Waxwings by Bob Comix/creazilla.com (used under a CCA 4.0 license)
Nuthatches by wectors/123rf.com
Creepers by cliker-free-vector-images
Gnatcatchers based on a photo by Mark R. Johnson
Wrens by Loveleen/stock.adobe.com
Catbirds, Thrashers & Mockingbirds based on a photo by Mark R. Johnson
Starlings based on a photo by Mark R. Johnson
Thrushes by Jackie/cleanpng.com
Finches by Stefanie Schubbert/shutterstock.com
Old World Sparrows based on a photo by Mark R. Johnson
New World Sparrows & Towhees by Noah Strycker/shutterstock.com
Meadowlarks, Orioles & Blackbirds by Birchside/gograph.com
Warblers by thesilhouettequeen/123rf.com
Tanagers, Cardinals & New World Buntings based on a photo by Michael Fish
Bald Eagle by Kiera Awayuki/iStock.com
Great Blue Heron by Skyworks2051/dreamstime.com
Hooded Merganser by Orxpikdesign/dreamstime.com and Creative Stall/shutterstock.com

BIBLIOGRAPHY

American Ornithological Society Checklist of North and Middle American Birds. 2024. American Ornithological Society. Retrieved from: https://checklist.americanornithology.org/taxa/

Behrens, K., and C. Cox. 2013. *Peterson Reference Guide to Seawatching.* Boston: Houghton Mifflin Company.

Birds of the World. 2025. Birds of the World: An ornithological research platform focused on the life histories of birds (website). Cornell Lab of Ornithology, Ithaca, New York. https://birdsoftheworld.org/bow/home

Dunn, J. L., and J. Alderfer. 2017. *Field Guide to the Birds of North America.* 7th ed. Washington, D.C.: National Geographic.

"Eastern Shore Bird & Wildlife Trail." 2024. Virginia Department of Wildlife Resources. Retrieved at: VirginiaWildlife.gov/BirdTrail

eBird. 2025. eBird: An online database of bird distribution and abundance (website). Cornell Lab of Ornithology, Ithaca, New York. ebird.org.

Ellison, W. G. (editor). 2010. *2nd Atlas of the Breeding Birds of Maryland and the District of Columbia.* Baltimore: Johns Hopkins University Press.

"Habitats of the Chesapeake Watershed." 2024. Chesapeake Bay Foundation. Retrieved from: https://www.cbf.org/issues/habitat/index.html

Kaufman, K. 1996. *Lives of North American Birds.* New York: Houghton Mifflin.

Maryland Biodiversity Project. 2025. Maryland Biodiversity Project: A non-profit organization focused on cataloging the living things of Maryland (website). https://www.marylandbiodiversity.com

Means, J. 2010. *Roadside Geology of Maryland, Delaware, and Washington, D.C.* Missoula, Montana: Mountain Press Publishing Company.

O'Brien, M., R. Crossley, and K. Karlson. 2006. *The Shorebird Guide.* Boston: Houghton Mifflin Company.

Sibley, D. 2014. *The Sibley Guide to Birds.* 2nd ed. New York: Alfred A. Knopf.

Solyst, J. 2020. “What Habitats Are Found in the Chesapeake Bay Watershed?” Chesapeake Bay Program. Retrieved from: https://www.chesapeakebay.net/news/blog/what-habitats-are-found-in-the-chesapeake-bay-watershed

Swanson, S. 2022. *Best Little Book of Birds: The Oregon Coast*. Portland, Oregon: Timber Press.

xeno-canto.org. 2024. A website for sharing recordings of wildlife, worldwide. Xeno-canto Foundation, The Netherlands. https://xeno-canto.org/about/xeno-canto

Xiong, Y. and C. Berger. 2010. “Chesapeake Bay Tidal Characteristics.” *Journal of Water Resource and Protection*. Vol. 2, pages 619-628. http://www.scirp.org/Journal/jwarp

Zimmermann, Joe. 2023. “Warming Temperatures Bring Different Animals to Maryland.” Maryland Department of Natural Resources. Retrieved from: https://news.maryland.gov/dnr/2023/10/10/warming-temperatures-bring-different-animals-to-maryland/

INDEX

C

F

G

H

I

J

K

L

M

N

O

V

W

Y

Z

MARTA COSTANZO YOUTH

HOWARD YOUTH has been birding the Chesapeake Bay region since the age of 12. A freelance writer and editor, he previously held editorial positions at conservation organizations including American Bird Conservancy, Friends of the National Zoo, and Worldwatch Institute. Howard also wrote for a variety of publications while living abroad in India, Spain, Ecuador, and Nicaragua. He is the author of *Field Guide to the Natural World of Washington, D.C.*

GEMMA RADKO has been an avid Maryland birder for over 30 years. She is a member of both the Montgomery and Frederick chapters of the Maryland Ornithological Society, and often leads bird walks. As a licensed bird bander, Gemma ran a MAPS (Monitoring Avian Productivity and Survivorship) banding station for nine years, and she now teaches introductory ornithology and other birding classes at Nature Forward in Chevy Chase, Maryland.

LOIS LEONARD